ACCLAIM FOR MARY T. WAGNER AND
"RUNNING WITH STILETTOS"

2008 SILVER FEATHER AWARD WINNER
Illinois Woman's Press Association
2008 Communications Contest

"From cookies to Harleys, Catholic school to country living, Mary Wagner wields a pen of steel that hides a marshmallow heart. Read these essays and try your best not to smile."

—Frank Joseph, author
TO LOVE MERCY

"Enthusiastically recommended..."
Midwest Book Review

FIRST PLACE AWARD, NON-FICTION
National Federation of Press Women's
2009 Communications Contest

"Funny, plucky, razor sharp, and occasionally heartbreaking, *Running with Stilettos* is a breezy, marvelous read. Wagner gives ingenious vent to the precarious balancing act of every woman's life, whether teetering fashionably in high heels or desperately mastering a cordless drill in wet, muddy sneakers."

—Leslie Talbot, author
SINGULAR EXISTENCE

"...a consummate wordsmith..."
GrowingBolder.com

HECK ON HEELS

Still Balancing on Shoes, Love,
and Chocolate!

Mary T. Wagner

iUniverse, Inc.
New York   Bloomington

HECK ON HEELS

Still Balancing on Shoes, Love, and Chocolate!

iUniverse books may be ordered through booksellers or by contacting:

iUniverse
1663 Liberty Drive
Bloomington, IN 47403
www.iuniverse.com
1-800-Authors (1-800-288-4677)

Because of the dynamic nature of the Internet, any Web addresses or links contained in this book may have changed since publication and may no longer be valid. The views expressed in this work are solely those of the author and do not necessarily reflect the views of the publisher, and the publisher hereby disclaims any responsibility for them.

ISBN: 978-1-4401-8165-8 (pbk)
ISBN: 978-1-4401-8166-5 (ebk)

Printed in the United States of America

iUniverse rev. date: Oct/30/2009

This book is dedicated to...

my children—Deborah, Sarah, Michael and Robert—

whose every breath gives lift to my wings...

and to the wonderful women in my life...

because from cradle to grave, it's our girlfriends we *really* grow old with!

Contents

Forward

I've still got sand in my shoes.

No, not the kind that Dido sings liltingly about in "Sand in my Shoes," with a music video of sun-drenched tropical vacation romance and a rueful return to reality while images of a tall, dark, and handsome stranger with great abs float lustfully through her memory.

This would be more the Midwestern beach variety, in fact, from a photo shoot in the dead of winter on the shore of Lake Michigan. Two days before New Years Day, 2007. While it would be incredibly exciting and adventurous to report that someone was using a camera to pose and take glamorous pictures of *me* for some reason, the gritty reality is that I was sunny-side down on the wet sand, stretched out full-length shooting pictures at eye-level of my favorite high heels with the waves breaking in the background. I was starting a blog, and I was calling it "Running with Stilettos," and I wanted a cute shoe picture to kick it off with.

I just hoped that nobody was watching! So much for launching a project with confidence and energy and a blaze of glory. I felt so ridiculous in this quest that I first left the shoes and the camera back in the car while I scoped out the beach for other signs of humanity. Once at the water's edge, I looked up and down the shoreline. The nearest people were at least two blocks away in each direction. Whew! I went back to the car, grabbed the gear, and got busy. Cold, and wet, and sandy, and busy.

But let me back up the truck here for a minute. I didn't know the first thing about blogging. I hadn't published a line that didn't involve a legal issue of some sort since I'd started law school ten years before. When I'd switched career horses from journalism to law at that point after a life-changing accident, I never thought I'd be missing it. And oh boy, was I wrong! While my life operated on entirely too much "chaos theory" to marshal focus and concentration for, say, writing a novel, friends finally convinced me that I needed an outlet for creative writing again, and steered me into setting up my own website.

I was a babe in the woods. I carbon date from the time that my journalism college had a room full of selectric typewriters for students to use for their assignments. In my first newspaper job, I had to be **ordered** to start composing a feature story on a computer keyboard instead of writing it out by hand on a legal pad first. Okay, enough of a trip down memory lane, I'm not as old as Santa Claus.

But this was a whole new world. I needed an endless supply of help navigating every step of the set-up process, and all I really knew was that I had one essay I wanted to write and hoped that more would follow. And I needed, in my mind's eye, a cute shoe picture. Fast.

The pre-launch day for the blog was gloomy and overcast for the most part, and I wondered how I was ever going to get this accomplished. Nobody was holding a gun to my head and saying "publish *now*." But I felt a devil-may-care new-beginnings quality to the timing of pushing the "print" button on New Year's Eve, and then heading out to ring in the new year with friends and champagne. The essay was already written, the structure of the website set up. I kept slogging morosely through the day with household tasks. Then suddenly the clouds broke up and I saw sunlight in my front yard, and I kicked into gear, throwing three pairs of my favorite spike heels and a camera into an Ann Taylor bag and heading to one of my favorite beaches thirty miles away.

Life is full of those serendipitous moments, as I keep finding out. I posed and snapped away, first the pink faux-alligator slingbacks, then the black leather numbers with the cream piping and perky bows, then finally the caramel colored faux-alligator stilettos. I worked really fast, not just because I didn't want anybody to walk by and alert the mental health authorities, but because my fingers were freezing. Convinced that there had to be a usable shot in one of the dozen I'd snapped, I stood up, packed my meager supplies away, and turned to walk back to the car. As I turned, I noticed that from this angle, the afternoon sunlight caught the waves in an entirely different way. A spasm of curiosity fired up.

Hmmm..... On the downside, I was cold, I was wet, and the bystanders (*gasp!*) were getting closer. On the upside, I was already covered with wet sand from my chest to the tips of my toes. And I was here. Out came just the caramel colored stilettos and the digital camera and I wiggled my fingers to get the blood circulating for just a little while longer. I flopped down on the sand one more time, and snapped all of two pictures before saying "enough already!"

You can guess how this story ends, of course. The last picture I snapped—of the two I had never set out to take—turned out to be the best of the bunch. Not only did it launch the blog, I used it for the cover of my first book, "Running with Stilettos." *And* my business cards. *And* the promotional postcards I still hand out shamelessly at every opportunity.

I don't think I'll ever entirely get every grain of sand out of the sneakers I wore to the beach that day. But I don't mind. I still look back in wonder at the workings of chance in our lives, and the fun to be had by following the sudden question "why?" with the reply "oh, *why the hell not???*"

I've found it to be a darn good theory for daily living.

And an even *better* theory when it comes to shopping for shoes...

Author! Author!

 Of all the accessories to bring along to my first ever book-signing, the rocks proved to be the most practical. I'd packed books, of course, and a couple of pens, sunblock and lipstick, even bought a package of emergency M&Ms when I stopped for gas on the way to Chicago. But in the final analysis, it was the rocks.

Yesterday was my maiden voyage into the realm of in-person book promotion. I was hanging out my shingle at the Printer's Row Book Fair, billed by the Chicago Tribune as "the Midwest's largest literary event." I'm lucky enough to belong to two press organizations, the Chicago Writers Association and the Illinois Woman's Press Association, that had tables or tents set up at the fair for members to display at. So off I merrily drove for my book fair adventure, with a forty-pound suitcase, a full tote bag, a purse, and a stand-up display.

But first, a word about the preceding frenzy of disorganization. As in every step of the way in this journey into print, opportunity has been racing far ahead of preparation, and I've been dog paddling as fast as I can to keep up.

The wardrobe malfunction was first on the list. For weeks I'd known what I was going to wear. I was wedded to the idea of my show-stopping pink spike-heeled sling-backs, and had the perfect summer dress to go with. Sleeveless, tropical, a little flirty with side slits at the hem, and with pink hibiscus flowers on a black background, above all, slimming. The afternoon before the fair, as I finally started to pack, I put on the shoes and then tried on the dress for the first time since last summer. Oops…big time. Somehow over the winter, my hips had re-sized themselves, and the dress was suddenly strategically inoperable. So that's where all those cozy mugs of Kahlua-spiked hot chocolate topped with whipped cream and nutmeg in front of a toasty fire went last winter. Darn!

Since the pink stilettos were non-negotiable, I tore into the nearby town, searching frantically for a comfortable figure-flattering summer dress with enough pink in the design to match the shoes. With the primary choices being Kohl's and a place called Dress Barn, I soon found out it was going to be harder than I hoped. I looked at the clock on the dashboard, calculated how many hours remained—three— before the man in my life showed up for dinner, gritted my teeth at the thought of getting snared in rush-hour traffic, then gunned it to an upscale mall in Milwaukee thirty miles away.

After searching pretty much every dress section in the mall at warp speed, there were two things I knew, as Oprah likes to say, "for sure." One was that I'm really picky about dresses. The other is that when clothing sizes get into the double digits—anything above, say, a size eight—vertical stripes do **not** make you look thinner. In the last store at the far end of the mall from where I'd parked, I settled on a sale-priced tropical print tunic with plenty of pink in it, to go over black slacks. Less expensive than the dangly earrings I then bought as a chaser...but both still cheaper than a dress.

I got home, tidied up the kitchen, started a load of wash, began stacking books in a suitcase, then checked on the Chicago weather for the next day. High winds, possibly the occasional thunderstorm. The man of my dreams took a long-enough break from shooting arrows in the back yard to fashion a couple of makeshift braces for the display from a pair of wire coat hangers. Nothing fancy for this gal at this precise moment, just something that worked. And didn't require another trip to town.

The display itself had come into being just a few days before, after I'd met Paul Salsini, a Marquette University journalism professor and fellow author for coffee. After giving me an insider's perspective on marketing tips and personal appearances, he'd counseled me on the need to have some kind of a promotional poster on display near the books. There was no time, of course, to remotely think about getting something professionally printed. But it's amazing what you can accomplish with a sheet of industrial strength cardboard, a can of "hammered copper" Rust-oleum, some frantic and experimental eight-by-tens at one-hour photo pricing, and a roll of camouflage duct tape.

The coat hanger braces raised another yet wind-related problem. What to do about the piles of promotional postcards I'd had printed up to casually hand out to passers-by? Set down without something weighing them down, they could end up in Kansas. The answer was a few feet away in the garage. I started rummaging through dusty cubbyholes for rocks the kids had brought back from fifteen years worth of family vacations at rocky shorelines, and came up with four. One looked like a flower with very thick petals, one was covered by tiny chains of fossils, one was a pretty chunk of quartz, and one just look like...a rock. The suitcase started to feel heavy enough to tie a body to and hide it in Lake Michigan.

I showed up at the fair, gear trundling behind me on wheels, feeling like Dorothy just arrived in Oz. Okay, okay, we know that Dorothy had a few rough days in Oz. Flying monkeys, the Wicked Witch, those weird talking trees that threw apples. I'm thinking more like the early happy scene where everything is strange and new and she gets greeted as the heroine of Munchkin Land while the Lollipop Guild and the Lullaby League sing for her. The book fair was enormous, with the treasure-seeking vibe of a bustling, bohemian flea market…but with an army of identical upscale tents stretching for blocks in a regimented row down Dearborn Street and around into Polk, accented by live music, table-top vendors, and reserved-seating venues for talks by big-name authors here and there. A vibrant, quirky little island of its own, in the midst of a vibrant big city. And my home town.

I found the IWPA tent, squeezed into my corner spot of the table I shared with two other gals, and started to unpack. The predicted "high winds" in the Windy City channeled down the high-walled corridor of Dearborn Street with the turbulent speed of rapids through a slot canyon, and it was instantly clear that despite the makeshift braces and duct tape, the poster was going to go flying if left unattended. I gamely stood for the next four hours with my arm draped casually across the top to hold it down. I didn't know I could do without a bathroom break for that long. I smiled, signed, chatted, passed out innumerable promo postcards, and wrestled with the wind to keep the poster on the table. I thanked heaven for the fact I'd eaten breakfast before I left, since the wind only let up for about twenty seconds, enough time for me to dash to the center of the tent and scarf down three donut holes before returning to my post.

Four hours later, it was time to move shop to the CWA table. This time I took down the poster for good and left it and the duct tape behind. This gig was a little more relaxed—without the poster, I could finally sit down. I still shamelessly and reflexively handed out postcards to anyone who made eye contact. A teenager looking too young to find the book interesting? "Here, bring one home to your mom!" A single guy of any age? "Here, take one for the woman you love!" One guy smiled and shook his head, remarking "well, that would be the man that I love." No problem. "Oh heck, I'm sure you've got a niece or a sister!" He took the postcard with and started to read as he walked.

Two hours passed in the blink of an eye, accented by the growling of my empty stomach. At nearly four, I remembered the "emergency M&Ms" in the bottom of the tote bag and tore into them gratefully, still working the crowd, one hand passing out cards, the other shoveling candy into my face, momentarily unable to make polite conversation with a mouthful of candy-covered chocolate.

At four, I made my way back to the big tent and started to pack up. Two hours were officially left for the fair that day, but the crowds had started to thin, and the folks that remained had that weary "I've been here too long and just want to go home" look in their eyes. The clouds got darker, and the wind picked up, and just as I closed the last remaining book into the suitcase, I saw umbrellas start to open in the crowd. I had picked as good a time as any to make a graceful exit. The gals sharing the table with me said that the paperweight rocks had worked like a charm, holding down the stacks of postcards I'd left behind which folks still stopped by and snapped up.

Other authors had plenty to tell me about what typically made a "good" day or a "bad" day for them at a book fair, but with nothing of my own to compare it to, I'd have to say I had a pretty fabulous day. I sold some books, signed some autographs, shook some hands, met some interesting people, tried something new. Talked about shoe shopping at length with a lively, ebullient couple visiting from New York, talked about law with a man whose son just finished his first year of law school and wanted a career in public policy, talked about writing with a young woman just starting out as an essayist, talked about large families with a young woman who was the fourth and youngest child in hers. Pointed out the exact page in the book where the word "sex" appeared—just once!—to a man who was thinking about buying it for his thirteen year old daughter. Met a neonatal intensive care nurse writing a series of suspense novels. Yeah, it had been a very, **very** good day.

I found the parking lot where I'd left the car, loaded the bag of books that were left into the back, and cautiously navigated a labyrinth of steep, narrow ramps back down to street level. As I pulled forward into the street, the rain started to come down in buckets. Then, still feeling a lot like Dorothy, I left the Land of Oz behind, and made my way through the storm to get back home.

Marsh Madness

 The price of gas was $3.96 a gallon at the pump up the street, and the inevitable question to be asked before I turned the key in the ignition was, "is this trip really necessary?"

The sun was shining and my good binoculars and weathered field guide to the birds east of the Rockies were in the passenger seat beside me. There was no shortage of stuff to do in and around the house on my day "off." I couldn't remember the last time I had sorted laundry. Papers— for work, for amusement, for health, for the kids, for taxes—kept multiplying in stacks every time I turned around and refused to file themselves. There were buttons to be sewn, dishes to be washed, socks to be sorted, dust bunnies to hunt down and exterminate.

And instead, I was heading out to the Horicon Marsh forty miles away to watch birds. Was this trip really necessary? Damn straight! Once in a while you just need to take a "mental health" day from routine.

I eased the car down the driveway, and headed west, satisfaction and anticipation and guilty pleasure jostling for supremacy in my mind.

The first time I saw this extraordinary place, I was in a suit, and in a hurry. I was driving about a hundred miles from the office after work to Madison, Wisconsin, where my daughter had a scholarship dinner. A bailiff at the courthouse, well versed in both travel and transporting prisoners, gave me directions for the scenic route that would also help me avoid traffic delays. I drove along, already exhausted from a day that had started with opening pasture gates and measuring horse feed at 5:30 a.m., and thought agreeably that the road less traveled was indeed scenic. And repetitive. There's a lot of Wisconsin that looks alike. Red barns, green grass, black and white cows, wooden board fences weathered to a three-dimensional silver sheen.

And then all of a sudden I rounded a curve on a downward hill, and the marsh spread out before me, shimmering in the afternoon sun, water and vegetation as far as the eye could see. Highway 49 cuts straight through the marsh from east to west, a two-lane ribbon of road bisecting the marsh just above water level, giving the feel of following Moses through the Red Sea. I took a ten minute detour to do the "auto loop" and then got back on track. I promised myself right then that I'd come back when I had more time to spend, and I have, making the pilgrimage a couple of times a year.

On this particular morning, I was still seeing plenty of the same barns, and grass, and cows, and fences. But a bumper crop of spring dandelions cheerfully accented the greenery like party favors. When I finally hit that straight stretch of Highway 49 flanked by water and big sky, the last leg before my cherished turn off, pairs of geese casually herded their broods of olive-yellow goslings along the road shoulders. They must have it down to a science, I thought, since the only roadkill around looked like dead deer. Red-winged blackbirds perched on last season's cattails and flashed their scarlet epaulets, resembling unregenerate escapees from a military academy.

Driving into the marsh (which fortunately has restrooms, parking lots, and hiking trails) is like stepping out of time and into the meadow and forest primeval. From the time the car door opens you're enveloped by a symphony of bird calls in surround sound, walls of joyous noise in a language we can't understand, but which communicate volumes anyway. Profusion is the key element, surrender the only path. Traffic noise falls far behind the deeper you drive and hike, until finally you are left with only the sound of branches bending, leaves rustling, and the occasional flutter and splash of wings on water, mysterious takeoffs and landings far different from ours.

Passing one side channel, I slowed to watch a sextet of painted turtles basking in the sunlight on a half-submerged log. Nearby, a blue-winged teal balanced motionless on one leg on another snag, his beak buried under his wing and his head almost hidden by his spotted chest.

I parked and took the boardwalk into the marsh, an experience impossible to forget. I left my cell phone in the car, slipped a camera into my jacket pocket instead. A Canada goose stood up from her mounded nest in the middle of the water, rearranged her eggs among the fluff surrounding them, and settled back down, her outstretched wings sealing in her warmth. Barn swallows and tree swallows swooped and dived, Mother Nature's versions of the F-15. A couple of American coots bobbed their way down another side channel, with a slow, measured cadence like elderly beachcombers passing the morning with metal detectors at the shore.

The boardwalk gave way to a trail cut through the woods, and watching for birds gave way to a different kind of discovery. On this particular day, the forest floor was carpeted in white trilliums and purple and yellow violets, with a few wild geraniums in the mix. Fallen trees and branches, covered with moss, made for structural mystery in the distance.

The sky looked like rain would be moving in soon, but I set out on another hiking trail, this one running through a meadow and some more woods. My favorite seat has always been a solitary wood plank bench with trees and lilacs behind it. Judging by the number of cars in the parking lot—two, if you counted mine—I was the lone human for at least a half mile in any direction. I exercised my prerogative of solitude and stretched out on the bench flat on my back. Took off my glasses, shut my eyes, and just listened. I was surrounded, I knew, by a cacophony of warblers, sparrows, wrens, juncos, who knows?

Can I identify birds by the sounds that they make? Absolutely almost never. I have a tin ear when it comes to bird calls. Can I even tell what I'm looking at without opening the field guide? Not too often, unless it's something I've seen a dozen times before. But I can still marvel at just how much sound can some from such tiny instruments…and still get a kick out of the fact that one of my feathered troubadours today sounded a lot like R2-D2 in "Star Wars."

Picking up the pace as the clouds rolled in, I entered the woods again. Surprised a doe as I was coming uphill around a turn in the forest. We both startled, but a few graceful leaps, her white tail upright like a flag, and she was invisible in her element once again.

I reentered the car, and the modern world of technology, just as the raindrops started to fall. Still, I stopped often on the road to the exit, turned off the engine, and just watched through the open window. A female summer tanager, brilliant yellow and pale green, flew to and from her nest in the fork of a tree branch. Pairs of geese floated along with their goslings between them, disappearing into the forest of cattails standing in the water when they felt too much attention was being paid.

Four and a half hours had passed from the time I left the house until the time I got back, more than three of them "on the ground" at the marsh. The laundry still sat in the baskets, the dinner plates still hadn't walked themselves into the dish washer, the cat had shed a half dozen more balls of fluff the size of small tarantulas around the living room, and the dog still looked at me with those sad eyes, telepathically communicating his reproach, "you don't spend enough time with me!" Never mind that "enough time" for this dog would be upwards of twenty four hours a day.

But still, in the grand scheme of how to spend four hours if you don't have a gun to your head or a wolf at the door…was this trip *really necessary*?

You bet your ass.

Riding Pillion

If I'd had a list of what I was looking for in a man, owning a motorcycle wouldn't have been down at the bottom, it wouldn't have made the list at all. Truth be told, it would even have tipped the balance the other way. I don't like loud engines. I have no sense of balance. I get dizzy on a step ladder if I'm a foot off the floor. I'm a control freak. And on and on.

But there I was, at the tail end of what I call "the year of turbo-dating," metaphorically ready to take a step back and enter a convent for a while. And then there he was. Intelligent, intriguing, good looking and unconventional, the proud owner of both a longbow and a Harley. And so I threw caution to the wind and said "yes" to a first date.

The motorcycle was such a non-issue at the time. I live in Wisconsin, and it was the middle of January. I can't remember if I wore long underwear on our first date, but I most certainly wore it on our second. Along with shearling-lined lug-soled boots, ear muffs, and an

Eddie Bauer goose down parka trimmed with coyote fur. The wind chill was twenty-five below zero that night as I drove to meet him for dinner and a movie, far removed from biking weather up here. We have potholes and boilerplate ice up here that can take out a car. I also remember taking stock of the ridiculously, dangerously cold weather and thinking "girl, you're in trouble here!" But still…most of my dating for the past year had been "catch and release" after the first encounter, and the "curse of the third date" still lurked out there. No need to worry about riding on the motorcycle months from now when we might be calling it quits over dessert.

By the time the warm days of spring finally rolled around, I'd been caught, hook, line and sinker. His enthusiasm for biking had always been palpable, but now it was edging into my future as well. I couldn't hang out on the tailgate of his pickup truck forever. I kept ducking the issue. But the day of reckoning finally arrived.

I'd offered to take him out to dinner to celebrate a life-altering, monumental gardening project we'd recently finished around my house. The gardening was his idea. The "before" looked like a wasteland. The "after" had me walking in beauty every time I stepped out the front door. In between, we'd shoveled about two and a half tons of gravel by hand together and replaced it with perennials and rose bushes and bark and sandstone. My life was forever changed.

And so, reluctantly, fearfully, holding tightly for dear life, I acquiesced and positioned myself to ride pillion, taking pains to not nick the gas tank with the heel of my boot as I swung my leg over. I wore a borrowed leather jacket, and a borrowed helmet, and couldn't bring myself to even look over his left shoulder at oncoming traffic. We made it to the restaurant and back alive. And as some old friends entered the restaurant and got acquainted with my guy before dinner arrived, I confess to a certain thrill at nodding at the motorcycle gleaming in the sunlight through the window, and saying "yeah, that's my ride!"

Both we and the bike are now a couple of years older, and quite a few more miles have passed beneath the tires of the Harley with me on board. I've gone out and bought my own black leather jacket, after finally coming to grips with the fact that my chest is bigger than his. I've become accustomed to looking over at what's on the left side of the road now, as well as just looking up at the clouds and the trees and the birds above me as the wind slides over my face. The smell of damp evergreens on a winding two-lane road is as intoxicating as any glass of champagne. Last summer I watched a flaming sunset sky unfold behind me in the rearview mirrors as we drove east into twilight. It was magic.

Life's been getting in the way of riding much lately. Details like basement flooding and roof repairs and replacing the ring gear on the lawn tractor can take a bite out of leisure time. And as we're well aware, both life and relationships hold no guarantees. But that black motorcycle jacket hangs in the closet nearest the front door, a reminder of miles spent already with my arms around his waist, circled by the familiar smell of pipe smoke and leather, and holding the promise of open road once again.

In terms of "take me away" moments…it sure beats a bubble bath.

The Volcano Diaries

"You can always turn back!"

Not the most encouraging advice ever given to a hiker thinking about setting off on a trek up the side of a dormant-but-active volcano where the trail began at more than 8,000 feet above sea level and the difficulty rating for the 2.4 mile hike in the national park pamphlet was "strenous."

Gulp.

But then, I really hadn't been looking for encouragement. I'd been looking for validation ... or any other form of an excuse to **not climb the mountain**.

My son and I were on a week-long traditional mom-and-me vacation on the West Coast, a trip of particular poignance because he's the last of the brood and his departure for college means my nest will be empty for the first time in twenty-eight years. We'd stopped at Lassen Volcanic National Park in northern California at the suggestion of a middle-aged couple we'd met at Yosemite when I volunteered to take their picture a couple of days earlier. I'd only planned for the first three days of the trip, figuring we'd make it up as we went along, and so we let ourselves be carried to higher altitudes on the descriptive phrases of our newfound acquaintances. This was my most wing-and-a-prayer vacation since I'd gone to Ireland for a month at the age of twenty-two with a backpack stocked with Carnation Instant Breakfast packets and a bicycle that I had to reassemble once I landed and the phone numbers of a few of my Irish relatives.

This time I was (much) older, and (much more) out of shape, and without the resiliancy of youth to cushion my missteps. And my left foot had been hurting like heck for the previous four months, making a reusable ice pack and a microwavable heat pack and a bottle of Advil part of my packing essentials.

My son and I had scoped out the park the evening before, after checking into our remote little motel that had been recommended on the fly two hundred miles before by the young man who had carved the bear I bought at a gift shop. Are we finding a theme here? One of the most memorable things my son said to me during the entire vacation was, stepping back into the motel room after phoning his girlfriend at twilight to chat, "Mom, I think I just heard a cow get attacked by a bear. Do you want to come outside?" What's a mother to say? Of *course* I stepped outside for a listen. And when the porch lights went out behind us, you wouldn't believe how fast we beat it back into the room!

But while he was outside on the phone, I'd been poring over the pamphlets and maps we'd picked up by the visitor center the night before. And by the time I went to sleep, I was convinced that between my lifelong acrophobia, and the troublesome foot, and the vivid description of altitude sickness that usually sets in ***at lower altitudes*** *than we were even going to start hiking at* I was going to chicken out in favor of a more leisurely walk half the distance to see a pretty waterfall.

All I was looking for when we pulled up to the park entrance the next morning was an excuse. I pled age, I pled infirmity, I pled forty extra pounds, I pled an appalling lack of stamina ... and then I threw in the vertigo and fear of heights for good measure. The heights thing is no laughing matter for me, in fact. I get dizzy if I climb higher than the first step on a ladder, and it's been like that for most of my life.

But the cheerful young lady in the Smokey the Bear ranger hat kept trying to steer me in the direction of optimism. Hikers of all ages and sizes were known to have made it to the summit, she said. Drink plenty of fluids to stave off altitude sickness. And remember, "you can always turn back." I didn't even have to turn my head to know that my son was grinning at the exchange.

We drove on to the base of the trail leading to Lassen Peak, topping out at 10,457 feet above sea level. We packed water bottles and granola bars and extra clothes in the backpack he'd be carrying. There were snow fields below where we even started. I felt out of breath at the first switchback, which was still so close to the parking lot it didn't even list how far we'd traveled. I wasn't going for glory here, just endurance, and so I just kept putting one foot in front of the other, watching my son's heels to keep from feeling dizzy just as I had hiking down the side of the Grand Canyon with my daughter a few years earlier. (It was a very character building experience.)

We met a delightful pair of teachers from Florida, Pat and Jackie, who went on hiking adventures during their summers off and decided to tackle Lassen this time. They each had a good dozen years or more on me, and were taking this adventure in stride. I didn't want to wimp out while they were watching, and so we overlapped each other's rest stops along the way up. They called out a lot of encouragement to me on the way up.

The higher we climbed, the more breathtaking the views became. The Sierra Nevadas were distant blue hills under a nearly cloudless sky. Lake Helen gleamed azure in the park below us. Snow fields were striped pink and white, but the air was still warm. The forests below looked as tiny as the shrubbery on a model train display. As we scrambled over loose gravel and larger rocks and tree roots, a doe picked her way across the side of the mountain above us, twin fawns scampering quickly behind her to the cover of some brush.

Continuing in the vein of being practical instead of heroic, I took plenty of rest stops along the way, chugging water and letting the faster hikers pass us by. And sometimes Pat and Jackie! There was usually a tree or two that I could sit under for shade, but inevitably we began to leave the tree line behind. Still, I kept going, watching my son's feet in front of me, occasionally getting a hand up over the rougher patches. And then, with less than a mile to the summit, I came to one more switchback and stopped. Up to my left, I could see the trail cross back and forth upon the bare mountain face. And to my right, I could see nothing but open sky.

Right then and there, my fear of heights suddenly nailed me to the side of the mountain. "Robert, honey," I said, "I'm sorry, but I just can't take one more step!" Of all the things that I thought would have shut me down long before—the extra pounds, the thin air at 9,000 feet, the gimpy foot—it was such an anticlimax to call it quits because of this!

Still, there was no going forward for me, and I sure wasn't going to go back down alone. I folded my fleece sweatshirt into a pad for my seat on a nearby rock, took custody of the backpack, and settled in to wait for my son to make it to the summit and bring back some good pictures. It took him two hours to get back, factoring in the half-hour phone call to his girlfriend from the top of the mountain, a lot of picture taking, and some time spent just glorying in the achievement.

As I sat, I basked in the sun and marveled at the grandeur surrounding me, and the total serendipity that had brought us here. Who knew, when we set out on this trip, that we'd be setting out to climb a mountain to its very top? Or photographing a yellow bellied marmot peeking out of his den near a set of volcanic vents? It was certainly an altitude on the side of a mountain that I never thought I'd experience.

A very long time ago, when a friend of mine was getting ready to leave college without graduating and faced a very uncertain future, I sent him on his way with an inspirational poster that read something to the effect that if you set your sights among the heavens, even if you fail you will fall among the stars.

I hadn't thought about that in quite a long time, but thought about it again recently. At the tail end of our vacation, we drove the well-maintained highway to the visitor center of Mount St. Helens in Washington state and realized that even though it looked rugged and awesome and high and imposing…we'd both made it farther above sea level than this national landmark.

But for me, an even bigger victory was just in getting as far as I had. I may not have made it to the top as I would have liked … but I ended up sitting high enough on the side of a mountain that I could nearly touch the stars.

Tough Enough?

The scene in the courtroom still haunts me ten years later.

I remember the tears that sprang hot to my eyes as I shut the door behind me and walked down the corridor, thinking "I am not tough enough to do this job." I was a law student then, a seasoned criminal prosecutor now. And from time to time, out of nowhere, still comes that memory. It is seared into my consciousness, a testament to "collateral damage," and a mother's grief—two mothers, in fact—and consequences reaped by horrific acts, and how nothing in life, either evil or good, ever happens in a vacuum.

But first, a bit about my job. For the past nine years I've been unbelievably fortunate to work as a criminal prosecutor in a part-time capacity. When I got hired, I felt like I'd hit the jackpot in terms of balancing life and work and family. I still do. I had four kids at home when I'd started law school, and still had three kids living at home when I finished. Getting to do the work I loved in a half-time structure meant that I could still make it to soccer practice and gymnastic meets and find the time to bake team cupcakes decorated like tennis balls and help with homework and volunteer at school and cook dinner on a regular basis. Okay, a semi-regular basis. My kids really got quite sick of "rotisserie chicken" and potato salad from the grocery store deli every Tuesday night.

This was a new position, not only for me, but for the District Attorney's office as well. And so little by little, my job duties evolved to make the most use of my time there and my previous background as a writer. While no one I work with would, I think, dare call me the politically incorrect "miscellaneous backup chick," I make sport of it myself. One cop, introducing me to another, described me as the office's "utility person." I have my areas of specialty—appellate work, child support prosecutions, seizing assets from drug dealers, responding to requests by inmates who are unhappy that their probation or parole has been revoked and want the trial court to overturn that administrative decision—and then I just get thrown into a lot of things with little warning. It comes with the job. I've argued four cases before the state supreme court, I've been admitted to practice before the United States Supreme Court...and I handle a lot of speeding tickets as well.

But being the part-timer means that for the most part, I don't handle the big cases from start to finish. I may review their police reports, I may issue the charges, I may even brief or argue a pre-trial motion, but I'm rarely there for the finish.

Ten years ago, I was simply a spectator in the courtroom. And it has stayed with me every step of the way since then.

A young man's life hung in the balance. His was the last sentencing hearing of a trio of young men who had, months earlier, kidnapped and savagely victimized a young woman in a highly-publicized case.

There were no reporters in the courtroom this time, no television cameras, no members of the public. Just the routine players in this type of drama. A judge, the defendant, a prosecutor, a defense attorney, the courtroom staff. And the families. Both his and hers.

His mother went first, a lioness trying to protect her son. She walked into the courtroom with a bearing that was so precise it was almost military. She was a flight attendant, and wore her navy uniform proudly, crisp white accents with glints of gold, her hair pulled severely back. The courtroom was a high security place, which meant that in addition to armed bailiffs being present as a matter of course, the "gallery" was separated from the court by walls of glass and wood. Sound was amplified and conveyed by microphone and speaker.

For nearly a half hour the young man's mother spoke before the judge, passionately pleading for mercy. Sometimes her voice was strong, sometimes it broke with emotion. In her hand she held copies of papers and artwork he had created in grade school that had hung on her refrigerator door years before. She told the tale of his life, which was in large part a tale of hers as well. Of a severely abusive relationship that she had finally found the courage to leave, of her struggle to claw her way out of a life of despair and establish herself as a professional in a field that leaves nothing to chance and relies on absolute accountability and responsibility. Her son's failings were not all his, she argued. He had been such a good child. But a cousin— one of the other defendants, in fact—had often led him astray as he was growing up. And she, in her job, had not always been there to counterbalance the influence.

And then the victim's mother spoke. The girl herself was not in the courtroom, but her mother and some other people were there to stand up for her. This mother was, on the outside, less crisply glamorous, more plain spoken than the woman who spoke before her. But she spoke eloquently about her child nonetheless, about a wonderful and responsible young girl who was the first in her family to go to college, who had a life bright and shining with promise and optimism. And whose life had been utterly broken by no fault of her own. Her daughter had had so much taken from her, and would never be the same. There needed to be justice here.

The prosecutor spoke then too, and the defense attorney, though I remember little of what either of them had to say. Real life and real heartaches trump the speeches of professionals most of the time.

And then it was the judge's turn. The words of the law fell heavily in the windowless courtroom. Punishment. Rehabilitation. Protection of the public. Concepts that judges apply every day in courtrooms across the country, elastic in their application but fixed in their importance as guiding principle.

But the moment that stays with me was one that was happening on the other side of the glass, in the gallery that separates the official participants in the case from everyone else. As the judge began to speak, the mother of the young man who had done such wrong walked around to the first row of the gallery, and knelt in front of the young woman's mother and put her hand on the other woman's lap. "I am so sorry," she said, and bowed her head, and then the two of them listened together for a verdict delivered in the pursuit of justice that would never make either of their children alright.

I fled the courtroom at that point, though not before hearing a sentence handed down which ensured that the young man would never see an ordinary sunlit day outside of a prison for most of his life, if not all. "I am not tough enough for this job," I thought as I wiped the tears away with my hand and then left the building.

It's been ten years since that day in the courtroom, nine years since I started working as a criminal prosecutor. I've had by victories and I've had my defeats, and none of them have shaken me to the core as much as this one did. I look back and still wonder whether I'm "tough enough" for the oath I've taken.

If I'm very lucky, I think and pray, I'll somehow make it to retirement before I ever find out.

The Feline Zone

 Living with a serial killer is starting to wear on me. After three consecutive mornings of stepping out of my bedroom and greeting the day by finding a fresh white-footed mouse corpse on public display, it's now the fourth day, and I haven't stopped looking around corners for yet another surprise.

Though I shouldn't have to look hard. He placed the last body at the foot of the front stairs, perfectly centered, front paws outstretched in death agony, head thrown back, perpendicular from head to tail to the edge of the bottom step. Hannibal Lecter in a fluffy fur coat when it comes to artful murder and postmortem staging. I pity those poor little mice who think they're moving to safety when they come indoors for the winter!

I didn't remember this much drama or bloodletting from having a cat when I was nine or ten. I recall one summer day when we had moved in temporarily with my grandparents, bringing the family pets. My grandmother was in the back room off the kitchen ironing a shirt when I let Tippy, our black and white shorthair, in through the back door. What I didn't know until then was that Tippy had a fat field mouse clenched in her teeth. The mouse wiggled free as soon as the door slammed, and my grandmother shrieked and flung herself across the ironing board to get her feet off the floor. Tippy pounced on the mouse, I pounced on Tippy as soon as she recaptured her prey, and I threw them both out the door. I still laugh at the thought of Grandma straddling the ironing board with her midsection. Lowbrow comedy, yes. Horror? Hardly.

We moved to a farm up north a few years after that, and I don't remember any fiendish "death art" scenes from our cats there either. I *do* recall looking across the farmhouse kitchen one day and spying a fat field mouse sitting atop a flour canister on the hutch next to the kitchen table, upright on his haunches and staring straight at me with an air of nonchalance. Obviously the cats we had back then didn't take their "search and destroy" missions too seriously.

My life was pretty much kitty-free after I left home for college a long time ago. Marriage to a man whose entire family was ferociously allergic to cats swept the idea of caving into the kids' pleas for a kitten every time one of their friends did right off the table. Twenty-five years later, though, divorce opened the door a crack…and then a canyon. Three days after I broke the news to my youngest son that his family was dissolving, he started to square his shoulders, get a little color back in his cheek, and look for a silver lining.

"Do you think that now we could maybe get a kitten?"

I smiled. He started to plot. At his urging, I began to call humane societies for kitten availability, but apparently it wasn't quite "kitten season" yet. To keep him out of my hair, I handed him the want ads. I was busy getting ready to paint a bedroom when my son, all of thirteen and more than a little reserved, came to me with an ad circled in the paper. He'd already made the call and had the first conversation with the owner. C'mon, Mom, please call this lady!

There was one kitten left, black with white paws and a white chest, in a small town, twenty five miles away. It was the day before Easter, and another buyer who sounded interested had already promised to come by. But still, she'd keep my number, and if this other person didn't show, we could stop by later that night. All the kids were home for the Easter weekend, and my soon-to-be-ex stopped by to pick them up and take them out to a custard stand for burgers. My son, ever the optimist, elected to stay home "to keep Mom company." Ha!

The "cat lady" called about ten minutes later. The earlier prospective buyer turned out to be a phantom, and the seller was out of patience. My son and I were in the car five minutes later with a written set of directions and a carrying case that most recently had been used to transport the rabbit to have his picture taken at a photography studio. That's another story.

As we rode along and the miles slid by, I voiced all the standard disclaimers. We were only going "to look." There were lots of other kittens out there somewhere to pick from if we didn't like this one. Animal shelters would soon be awash with spare kittens. We were *not necessarily going to buy this kitten!!!* My son nodded and kept on smiling, his grip tight on the carrying case, his excitement and anticipation an electric, palpable third occupant in the car. As I drove, I realized that unless this kitten had only three legs and a really bad case of mange, we were coming home with this cat. Dear God, please let it be a good one!

As expected, the kitten was tiny and frisky and healthy and adorable. Short-haired too, but appearances later proved to be deceiving. Twenty-five dollars later, the three of us were in the car for the ride home. We stopped at Wal-Mart for a litter box and some Tidy Cat before we even set foot in the house. My son spent the following week of Easter break largely cuddling and man-handling the newest member of the family, with the result that the kitten soon came to regard him as his new mother.

That was four years and sixteen pounds ago. Smokey, as we soon named him, has been altering our routines and our lives ever since. When he grew bigger than the rabbit and started looking at his fuzzy, spotted friend like he might be on the dinner menu , the rabbit went to the local Humane Society. When my daughter brought her new kitten home from college for eight months until she could find a new cat-friendly apartment, the two cats eventually reached a detente… but not before shredding the bedskirt of my new comforter set. When his long, fluffy, black gossamer fur started collecting on the bottom of the creamy white semi-sheer curtain that screened off the big bay window from the road and gave us a little privacy, I recognized a losing battle when I saw one and cut my losses. The curtains came down. I didn't think it was possible for a single cat to produce so much hair… but I soon learned otherwise after the vacuum cleaner intake hose got jammed up, and the utility sink in the basement overflowed from a clogged drain.

Smokey has staked his claim on the furniture as well. His favorite seat these days—when he's not curling up on one of our laps—is an antique overstuffed chair with carved hunting dog heads sprouting from the arms instead of knobs as ornamentation. My father-in-law had collected several of these chairs in his years of antique hunting, and had restored two of them for us. My ex and I spent **ninety-five dollars a square yard** on the woolen tapestry we picked for the upholstery, which with medieval-styled rabbits and deer romping on a field of navy and bunches of flowers, would have looked right at home at Windsor Palace. Smokey has reserved the chair nearest the crossroads of dining room and living room, and sits preternaturally upright in repose, one arm stretched the length of the armrest, his paw stopping just short of the carved dog head, looking for all the world like a corpulent Orson Welles in those old Paul Masson wine commercials. Adding insult to injury, he's commandeered my favorite pillow as well—velvet backed, with an elaborate needlepointed scene of scarlet-coated fox hunters on thoroughbreds clearing a hedgerow under a bright blue sky. You must admit the cat's got good taste. I derive some dregs of comfort by reminding myself that the chair was never all that comfortable to sit in anyway. And when was the last time I'd *really* used the pillow?

With my son getting ready to head off for college in a few months, it's been dawning on me recently that I'm going to have the equivalent of a heavy, warm, fur-covered boat anchor in my lap every time I sit down on the sofa for the next fifteen years. Nice on a cold winter night when there's a chill in the living room when there's no fire in the grate, not as wonderful when you're trying to slice into a pork chop while you watch "Law & Order" reruns with your feet up. Even more, though, it's going to be fifteen years of living with an inquisitive, unpredictable, languid, affectionate, unreadable and occasionally sadistic intelligence that's never boring.

The man in my life describes watching a bonfire at night instead of television as "only one channel, but it's always changing." I can safely say that Smokey's got his own single channel going as well, and it hasn't gotten boring yet. And until he decides to quit showing off the spoils of war instead of eating them…I'm just going to have to keep watching my step.

Alles Klar

I thought briefly about packing the shotgun, but the car was nearly full and I was exhausted with 120 miles yet to drive. Having any sort of a weapon in a house with an elderly ex-soldier with dementia issues never sounds like the brightest of ideas during daylight, no matter how "dodgy" the neighborhood. I also left the chain saw behind. Not that I'm sure I couldn't find a use for it...

The car was packed to the brim with my vacuum cleaner, the tool kit (with hex wrenches AND flat head screwdrivers), the cordless drill, extra plates and silverware, clothes for colder weather than the night I'd blasted down to Chicago like a bat out of hell, extra movies on DVD, my latest Oprah magazine, winter jacket, gloves and, of course, my Swiss Army knife which had already been pressed into use. And don't forget the plain black suit and heels, equally appropriate for either a funeral or a court appearance. Next stop, a nearby hardware store for a replacement part for an ancient broken doorknob, a fillup at the local gas station where regular unleaded goes for fifty cents less a gallon than it does in Chicago, a pitstop at Starbucks for some caffeine and a comfort zone, and a cruise through the racks of Best Buy looking for DVDs of Lawrence Welk and the Jackie Gleason show. Didn't find 'em, but at least I tried.

When I finally pulled out of the driveway, the late afternoon sky was starting to darken, heralding temps below freezing just ahead. The setting sun blazed gold from behind swaths of grey and silver clouds to the west, while the three-quarter moon glared brightly like a chunk of ice in the clear eastern sky. Squadrons of geese flew overhead, and a hawk soared over the interstate, utterly unconcerned with the myriad human dramas unfolding below him at seventy miles an hour on six lanes of traffic.

I was headed back to Chicago, my home town, for the worst of all possible reasons. The first frantic dash had been a few days earlier. One minute I was sitting at my desk at work, pushing my way through a neverending pile of paper. The next my cell phone rang with the news that my elderly mother, already in a wheelchair most of the time, had fallen and badly fractured a femur. My equally elderly father, incredibly feeble and showing symptoms of both Parkinson's and cognitive impairment, needed full-time care and supervision while the medical crisis unfolded.

And so I went, and waited, and talked with doctors and social workers and administrators and nurses, and tried to reassure my father that all would eventually be well. This last was a Herculean task. He and my mother had shared the same apartment for thirty years, and his anxiety was palpable.

In the coming days, I tag teamed him with my mother's two sisters— one with a game leg and a psychotic Dalmatian, the other, younger, married to a former firefighter who, in his eighties, proved to be the

Rock of Gibraltar every evening as we showed up at their house for dinner and a movie like orphans in a storm. With my father's limited mobility and attention span, we've watched a lot of TV and movies. Took in Gunsmoke episodes, laughed at the Three Stooges, guffawed at the mud-splattered antics of George Clooney and his football team in "Leatherheads." I tried hard to find movies in German, his native tongue, but turned up only two. One, "Schultze Gets the Blues" was so slow paced we switched it off. But not before he surprised me by singing along in German with the characters in a scene where some miners were being congratulated on their retirement.

We also watched Wolfgang Petersen's wrenching WWII epic "Das Boot" again, which we had first shared last summer when he visited. Seeing it again reinforced my twin beliefs that (1) the movie is a genuine classic with a thrilling, haunting musical score, a "must see" for film buffs even with only English subtitles, and (2) the actor playing the stoic, nuanced submarine commander, Jurgen Prochnow, is the most compelling actor I've ever seen on screen. And that includes Russell Crowe in "Gladiator," Viggo Mortenson in "Hidalgo," and Cary Grant in just about anything.

Just to get out of the house one day for a destination that didn't involve the hospital, I loaded him into the car and we visited the Garfield Park Conservatory, reveling in a riot of exotic chrysanthemums and bizarre succulents and lush foliage. We stopped for a while by the indoor pond populated by a colorful variety of ornamental carp and decorated with enormous glass waterlilies by the artist Dale Chihuly whose thousands of colorful glass flowers also famously grace the ceiling of the lobby of the Bellagio Hotel in Las Vegas. I restrained myself from physically yanking the trio of folks seated in the only bench near the water, and reminded myself that I was lucky to be here at all.

We drove through Humboldt Park in the old neighborhood, where I used to bike and swing and sled as a child and he and I searched for lost marbles on our walks in the woods. We cruised past the fieldhouse and the park's formal gardens and pool flanked by the pair of magnificent bronze bison originally designed for the 1893 World's Fair by Edward Kemeys, the same sculptor who created the signature giant lions guarding the staircase of Chicago's Art Institute. As we drove through the park, he recalled the neighborhood bakery, Rosers, and so we stopped there too, buying a loaf of rye bread and a butter coffee cake smothered with icing. Our drives here and there were often spent just listening to music, but sometimes he would give me a short impromptu lesson in German. I would have to lean close to hear him, because his speech is no longer clear.

My mother continues to improve, and the next days are fraught with uncertainty as to the future for both. But every night, as I have since this crisis began, I tuck him into bed with the words "Guten nacht, mein Papa." Then I kiss him on the cheek and tell him "alles klar." Roughly translated, it means "everything's fine." He smiles and closes his eyes and I turn out the lights.

Alles klar. At least for this night.

Grow, Dammit!

One popular definition of insanity is that of doing the exact same thing over and over, but expecting a different result.

This might explain why for three summers in a row, I've planted blue butterfly delphiniums in the same spot in my garden, only to watch them die off. And I'm still pondering whether I should to run to the nursery and buy three more in four-inch pots...for the same exact place.

To be fair, I'm sure they had help on the way to their Valhalla of the Verdant. I have rabbits in abundance, little Peter Cottontails romping around the yard without the blue jackets. I have a chocolate lab that likes to dig at the roots of plants where I've sprinkled dried blood meal to repel the rabbits. I have little striped gophers who scramble in and out of the drain pipes for the rain gutters that empty into both sides of the garden. The frantic scratching of their tiny feet inside the metal pipes as I round the corner is a gentle reminder that out in the country, you're never alone. I've been known to neglect watering, neglect weeding, neglect fertilizing, neglect spraying. Are you sensing a theme here?

But still. Other things abound, and in fact reproachfully encircle those pathetic empty spaces. The line of strawberry plants that run along the front of the garden have sent out tenacious masses of tendrils in each direction like a Roman gladiator hurling a net over an opponent in the Coliseum. I have to pull and rip and hack them into submission. The coneflowers behind them are sinking sideways from the sheer weight of their tangerine and yellow and white flowers. The hot pink phlox with the bi-colored leaves—a prized find at Home Depot last year—are ready to burst.

And yet, for whatever reason, the delphiniums have perished. Repeatedly. And yet, I recall their brief, glorious bloom the first year I put them in, and I still hope.

This is the third summer since the man in my life showed up with a pickup truck full of mulch and music and the enthusiasm for transforming 200 square feet of bare gravel-covered plastic akin to Michelangelo eyeing the ceiling of the Sistine Chapel. In just a few weeks, the fuse had been lit, an oasis born, a garden begun in my soul.

Planting a garden is such an act of faith! And in my case, blind faith. Where others may plan and coordinate colors and heights and growing seasons, I still take a more devil-may-care approach. Approximation was, and still is, my watchword. The only thing that I usually expect now is that if I put a plant in the ground, it will grow, at least for a little while. That's a big step up from the pre-gardening years.

There have been a few surprises along the way. **Who knew** ... that the little clump of "obedient plants" my gardening friend Rosemary shared with me, a tidy and demure two feet tall at the end of their first season, would spread like a virus and double in height, shading everything behind them like Godzilla looking down at a Manhattan subway station? **Who knew** ... that the white butterfly bush that I planted that first gardening season "just to keep him happy" would flourish like a spray of fireworks and make the view from across my ironing board such a delight as hummingbirds and butterflies and hummingbird moths looking like tiny flying shrimp hovered delicately and landed? **Who knew** ... how personally and even *parentally* involved I could feel as my little charges took root and grew ... or not. Hopes raised, then dashed, as sunflower and coneflower sprouts grew from seeds in peat pots in the house, then flourished for a few days in another new garden, then were nipped in the bud, so to speak, by the double whammy of the gopher next door and a finicky doe who didn't think the other fifteen acres of vegetation had quite enough variety for her palate.

I never imagined, in my wildest dreams, how much suspense and satisfaction could be sparked by finding a broken off stalk of sedum sitting on the checkout counter of the local plant nursery last summer. As a general rule, I don't even **like** sedum. But this forlorn amputee was both unusual and gorgeous, with sage green foliage edged in cream, and a large raft of tiny white and fuschia flowers on top. "Good lord, that's gorgeous," I commented to the clerk as she rang up my purchase.

"Why don't you take it home," she replied. "Just stick in the ground and see if it'll grow." I needed no further urging, and did as directed. Watered, and hovered, and watered, and hovered some more. By the time of the first frost weeks later, it hadn't grown any...but hadn't withered and died either. Post-winter, as the snow receded, I was back in the garden taking inventory, pushing away the mulch to see if all my babies had come back. The delphiniums didn't make it, but there at the site of the sedum stalk, was a tiny white bud just breaking through the soil. Eureka!!

There's not that much planting that will take place for the rest of this year. The challenge right now is just to beat back the weeds and remember to water through the dry spells of late summer. Even my watering technique has evolved into a tranquility zone of sorts over the past three growing seasons. Where I used to drag the hose from plant to plant to efficiently dump a gallon or two on each at a time, I now pull up a lawn chair on the parking pad nearby and sit and spray from a distance, remembering all the heat and dripping sweat and optimism and romance and pipe tobacco and sore muscles and music that went into creating it in the first place, as the leaves and stalks and flower heads bend gently under the cascading droplets.

That gorgeous sedum plant is just about ready to flower, and I'm no longer hovering like a demented soccer mom on the sidelines (*been there, done that!*). But something tells me that before the week is out, I'll be back at the nursery looking for another trio of butterfly blue delphiniums. And as I dig them into the garden, I'll be muttering both words of encouragement … and telling them to "grow, dammit!!"

The View from the Edge

I sit on a bluff overlooking Lake Michigan, the breeze smelling of pine resin and green things and earth and damp and summer heat. A hundred feet below me, the water is a roiling sheet of molten silver, a moving picture framed in lacy pine boughs. The wind fractures the surface crosswise as it touches down and the shimmering reflection scatters, the texture suddenly like dull ripples of sand. And then the wind stops for an instant, and the sunlight gleams off the water again, illuminating the flat limestone slabs just inches below the surface.

The motion is constant, undulating, tumbling, primeval, utterly hypnotic. An occasional seagull breaks the visual plane, its wings and back a silver grey like the waves, it's belly and throat white like the foam when they break.

A two-foot garter snake the color of leaf litter glides unhurried toward me across a carpet of pine needles and moss. Then he thinks better of his trajectory, bends right, and disappears in measured fashion over a tree root and down the bluff.

It is not "silent" here. The wind and waves and shivering birch branches above make that impossible. But is nonetheless quiet. A wonderful stillness for the soul. With the cell phone turned off and left behind in the log cabin, with no faxes, no sirens, no ambient traffic noise or squeal of brakes or crashing bumpers or barking dogs or skidding tires…with the roar of the wind above and behind me and the waves crashing below, I can hear my own thoughts again. And feel the music in my heart.

Home Fires Burning

The fruits of my labor were going up in smoke. In fact, they couldn't burn fast enough to suit me.

My ex-father-in-law (a good man still dear to my heart) was fond of saying that cutting firewood "warms you twice." Once from burning it in your fireplace, and once more from cutting it up in the first place.

With all due respect for age before beauty, I'd like to add to that list. At the moment, I could truly say that I was feeling mighty warm in the sunshine as I lugged the neatly cut pieces of firewood—harvested from another dead tree the wind had knocked down the night before and spread across the front yard—uphill in a wheelbarrow to the wood rack in the garage. Later, I knew, I'd feel positively toasty if not blast-furnace scorched as I set a match to the pile of broken and splintered branches that comprised the leftover trash from the wind's handiwork and stood by to keep a watchful eye on the blaze, raking smouldering logs and sticks from the edges to the glowing center of the fire.

And last, warmth of a different sort—the cockles of my heart feeling a glow of satisfaction as the horrible, thorn-covered, scratch-inducing, virally opportunistic trash trees I'd cleared out hissed and popped and shrank to glowing ash. Viewed with clinical detachment, in the war of woman vs. wilderness, the wilderness is winning. But at this moment, the goddess of fire tending strikes again, at least momentarily winning one skirmish in an ongoing war against forest succession in the form of twisted, blood-drawing, spike-covered brush rivaling anything ominously guarding Sleeping Beauty's castle in a fairy tale. Fairy tales don't live here anymore. Though I may change that tune someday when grandchildren enter the picture.

I've come late to this primitive source of elemental amusement combined with necessity. With fifteen acres to keep tabs on, a good man with a gasoline-powered chain-saw, and a pint-sized chain-saw of my own, I've been a fast learner.

One of the first rules of engagement is that, in the words of my Harley riding Muse, "you can burn just about anything if you've got enough lighter fluid." A few others are no brainers: keep a hose nearby and turned on; don't leave the fire unattended. And something I don't remember learning in Scouts, if the wind is blowing toward the house…close the windows before you get started.

But as with any utilitarian passion, there are graces notes that can elevate the gritty and necessary to the nearly sublime. A comfortable lawn chair, and a side table for a drink or two. Music makes it better by a quantum leap—a radio plugged into a socket in the garage, a boom box with a CD player if you're motivated enough to get up, strip off the work gloves and change the menu once in a while.

The binoculars usually come out as well. As the conflagration started to dwindle in the afternoon to more restful proportions, I sat and looked skyward more often. A red-tailed hawk circled above the woods behind the garage, the afternoon sun gleaming off his chest and the underside of his wings. Turkey vultures rode thermals high above, their black and grey wings tipped upward like Vs, wing tips spread like fingers arched back in pleasure. A pair of Canada geese flew past, so near to the ground I could hear the "flut, flut, flut" of their wingbeats. A robin played tug-of-war with a worm on the far side of the yard. In the distance, someone fired up a chain saw and I smiled to myself.

Not all the burning going on at my place is just about cutting firewood and clearning out brush. There are days, like this one, when I'm burning down the past as well. After a quarter century of marriage, I'm still getting my bearings in doing things on my own, setting my own course, claiming my own space, owning my own heart.

Every piece of scrap lumber that I drag out of the garage and pitch into the flames feels like a celebration of moving forward. Of putting to rest a traditional division of duties and stifled suggestions, of the time when the garage was "the man zone" and I simply parked my car there, of when the kitchen was "the female zone" and my critical thinking skills regarding the house pretty much boiled down to making a better cake and picking out wallpaper. Now I've got my own cordless drill and I'm not afraid to use it. If there's a leftover table leg or scrap two by four that I can't imagine using, pretty soon it'll be up in flames. And while the fire licks greedily at its new, ephemeral source of power, I can feel not only the old patterns of the past going up in smoke, but any bad feelings too. Lifted skyward on shimmering waves of heat and white smoke, to evaporate and then disappear.

I stepped away from the fire for a few minutes to walk through my garden, brand new last year, again the promise of flowers where there had once been an austere, lackluster field of white gravel. There were signs of life even in the middle of April when the last of the five foot high snow piles melted to grayish bumps in the lingering pockets of shade.

Early blooming Japanese peonies sent up red shoots on the south side of the house, inches from the last of the snow, promising intoxicating fragrance only a month away. There were buds on recently uncovered roses, coral bells and tiny, fragrant sprigs of lavender, foxgloves and holly hocks, sharp blades of daylilies, irises, feverfew, daisies, optimistically surging out of the earth despite the certainty that, in this part of the country, snow is surely just around the corner even though the flip flops and shorts have come out of storage.

I was burning solo this time. Two days of unseasonable near-seventies temperatures had driven me outside and away from the laundry (okay, to be honest did I really need an excuse at all?), out to the yard instead in leather work gloves and a tank top, wheelbarrow and hand saw and chainsaw in arm's reach.

Bonfires in the past year have usually been a joint endeavor, a hot twist on what otherwise would be "date night" if we weren't too tired and grimy from all the yard work that created that "burn pile" in the first place. There's something intoxicating and deliciously warm about sharing a chore, a kiss and a drink, and a sense of total but tangible, worthwhile exhaustion earned with pure, hard, muscle aching work. The "bonfire dates" have happened less often than I'd like lately—a result of poor timing combined with snow, rain, cold, wind, and teenage schedules. But I know the long, warm evenings of summer are just around the corner.

As afternoon segued into evening, my son returned from his weekend with his dad and sauntered into the yard. He finds watching a bonfire as mesmerizing and soothing as I do, and he quickly set to dragging more branches toward the fire pit and gathering armfuls of dead stalks that went up like tinder. We burned, and laughed, and talked, and caught up on the past couple of days.

Then as darkness fell, the fire died down to a pile of coals. I took the hose and sprayed the outer edges and grass surrounding the fire pit, and we headed indoors to make dinner and watch TV. Before we turned in, I raked the pile of dwindling coals down once more and gave one more good spray with the hose around the rim. In the total cloaked darkness of night in the country, a few lone embers gave off a feeble red glow, as if to say they would not go quietly into that good night.

It felt good to know the home fires were burning.

Breathing Space

 It was my second trip to the lakefront in under six hours. The first was a lunch-hour dash to the nearby harbor, slipping into the "emergency sneakers" I keep under my desk for just such occasions. I combined it with a trip to the gas station and a "drive through" at the post office with a quick hike along the breakwater, dodging patches of wet seaweed and fresh puddles for some exercise and a couple of stretches before heading into court for the afternoon. One of the many reasons I love where I work...but still, just a cruelly short taste of the magic of the shore.

On the way home, though, a phone call from my son about a violin lesson made me realize that he wouldn't expect warmed up spaghetti leftovers until at least eight. And so, as the exit to the state park on Lake Michigan loomed near, I recognized that the evening was warm and it was yet daylight and I had still had the chance to go barefoot at the beach and not get frostbite. *Carpe diem.* Who knew when I'd have another opportunity as effortless and spontaneous as this one?

I put on the turn signal and exited stage right, leaving the interstate behind in favor of a two lane country road to heaven. It's that time of year again. Squirrels and chipmunks busily gather and store nuts for winter, guys who love engines start tuning them up and getting them ready to face the cold weather, and I just try to stockpile as many glorious days in the waning sunlight as I can to tide me through the coming months of short, dark, snow-filled winter. Bah humbug!

I paid my five dollar entrance fee for an hour-long pass to the state park. Judging by the fact I still had my annual 2007 park sticker on the windshield, a full year had gone by since I'd been here last. The past year's been a pretty wild ride. A handful of bikers and hikers were just leaving as I pulled into the closet parking stall at the beach. I peeled out of my shoes, grabbed a blanket from the back seat, and left the cell phone in the car.

It was just me and the seagulls. The soft, white sand was crisscrossed by hundreds of their webby footprints. The gulls gathered at the edge of the water, facing into the wind with a rank-and-file military precision. Now that Labor Day has come and gone, humans are scarce on the beach these days. I set the blanket down in the lee of a stand of beach grass, and dug my toes into the cool sand. The water was a shimmering, iridescent blue taffeta with silvery grey undertones. White waves and cross currents broke in airy froth that caught the setting sun. The horizon was broken only by a small sailboat in the distance. I still had a half-cup of coffee from Starbucks left, and the warmth I felt on my insides as I swallowed made for a nice balance with the cool breeze off the water. The seagulls watched me but kept their distance, apparently able to discern that a coffee cup alone without a picnic basket beside it would yield no prizes worth taking flight or scrapping over.

I sat, hypnotized as usual, by the rise and fall of the waves and the low, constant roar of their crashing. Like listening to the world breathe. No easier way that I know of to let your mind break free from the worries and burdens that usually dog every routine step. I think growing up in Chicago has a lot to do with it. When your fondest childhood memories involve sand and waves and sunlight and the smell of Coppertone, I don't think you ever lose that primordial hunger for the nearness of endless water and a horizon without limits.

The shadows from the woods behind me eventually lengthened and overcame the shore, and the whitecaps no longer gleamed brightly in the sun. I didn't need a watch to know it was finally time to go. I drained the last of my coffee, shook off the blanket and made my way back to my car. It was still the only vehicle in the lot, looking like a shiny bright blue toy in an acre of striped asphalt.

As I left, I picked up a few white seagull feathers to take home to the cat. I'm sure he would have preferred a live mouse...but at least this would smell like some real prey. Then I nosed the car out of the park and back toward civilization, smiling all the way home.

Of Men and Mice

I grasped the tiny mouse mummy by the tail, between thumb and forefinger, and dislodged him gently from his final resting place. This corpse happened to be folded over a fan blade in the hood overhanging the kitchen stove, so there was a distinct 90 degree crease in his midsection. Still, he was dessicated and featherlight and otherwise as straight as a piece of balsa wood, and if I'd been so inclined, I could have amused myself trying to balance him tail-first on the tip of my finger.

My reaction wasn't a macabre juggling act, though, and so instead I pitched him without ceremony into the toilet, flushed, and returned to the stove where I flipped the "on" switch for the hood fan and heard it hum to life for the first time in at least six months. And noted again the amusing, sometimes infuriating, and ultimately bedeviling differences between men and women.

I'm no expert on the subject. Philosophers, writers, poets, artists, psychologists, Dr. Phil, Dr. Ruth, and the guy who wrote "Men are from Mars, Women are from Venus" have all run with the ball on the subject from the time "woolly mammoth with assorted greens" was on the dinner menu.

What had me laughing and grateful on this day, though, was the simple fact that no matter what problem I may be facing, and what machinations I may be thinking through to solve it, the reaction from the men in my life has usually been… "let's open 'er up." And so there's where we'll start…

The question, posed over coffee one morning to the man in my life, was simple and straightforward. "So what do you think would be involved in replacing the hood fan over the stove?"

The fan hadn't worked for at least a half a year, perhaps longer. One day it worked as well and dependably as it had for every day of the previous twenty five years. And then one day it just stopped. Not a snap, not a sizzle, not a groan. Just stopped. Leaving me to try to cook very carefully without spilling anything on the burners, because the resulting smoke had no place to go except out the kitchen window or the rest of the house. And with the cold weather setting in, opening the window over the sink and fanning the smoke out with a dish towel was getting old.

So the question was legit. My instinctive response when something old gets broke is to figure out where to buy a new one. So the questions followed in quick succession: What do these things cost? Could I pick one up at Menards or would I have to go to an appliance store and shop for one? Would installing it be fairly simple? Would I need an electrician to put it in? What, basically, would the job take?

The answer was a laconic "well, about an afternoon and a whole lot of swearing." But first, of course, there was the inevitable "let's take a look."

We looked. Peered around at the dimensions, tried to figure where the air logically vented out, studied how it was attached to the wall. Visions of installation costs, a strange electrician in my kitchen, possibly a new stove to match the hood fan as long as I was out shopping, and how to finance it all, danced in my head.

Then, the inevitable words, "let's open 'er up" came out, and I stood back as the testosterone in the room took charge. In about fifteen seconds the metal screen was off the fan, the unfortunate mouse came into view, the intractable obstacle was removed, and the fan was up and running again.

And I was suddenly reminded of a similar scene a few months before, involving a broken vacuum cleaner. An older upright model had quit working one day, and rather than look into getting it repaired right before company showed up for Thanksgiving dinner, I drove to a nearby Kohl's and bought a new one. It worked just fine for about a year, until the day I accidentally drove it over a sock in the laundry room while my attention was diverted elsewhere, and the smell of burning rubber and other drastic things mechanical brought me back to earth. The death of the machine was sudden. One moment it sucked stuff off the floor, and the next it did not.

I pondered yet another shopping trip in the coming weeks, as the leavings from the long-haired cat and the co-dependent retriever started to collect in the corners. But I happened to mention it in passing to that self-same man in my life not long after, and one night he showed up with a bottle of wine and his tool kit.

"Let's take a look," he said, and he patiently undid the bottom of the vacuum cleaner. "The belt's broken," he pointed out. An impromptu, immediate trip to Wal-Mart up the street turned up a replacement belt for a few bucks. It looked like a giant rubber band. Not exactly rocket science. By the end of the evening the machine was up and running and sucking down cat fluff again.

And I was truly amazed. My awareness of the fundamental differences between us had dated back to the birth of my sons. Up until that point, I had kinda, sorta bought into the theory that if you give kids of different sexes the same upbringing and the same influences, they grow up with pretty much the same impulses and reactions and priorities. That was until my older son was about two. At bedtime by that age, my daughters had been content to cuddle in my arms while I read them a story as The Sandman finally caught up with them. For my son it was different. I was a tall object to be scaled, a peak to be conquered. Not content to simply be held, he fasted all four limbs around me like a starfish clinging to a rock, every inch of body language wordlessly staking a primordial, possessive claim of "this is MINE." And if that wasn't enough, one night he rested his cheek against the sweater I wore, deemed it too scratchy, and imperiously directed, "I want you be SOFT!!"

Okaaaaaayyyyyyyyyy.............

I have been slowly getting initiated into some of the basics of "the man zone." Due entirely to the patient influence of a certain guy I know, I can now tell the difference between a hex wrench and a hammer, a putty knife and a pliers. And the importance of keeping the chain on your chain saw well-oiled lest it otherwise start "grabbing" while you're out cutting logs.

In fact, just a couple of months ago, I decided to personally take a screwdriver to that first broken vacuum cleaner sitting in the basement and check out a theory. Sure enough, it had stopped working because it had...a broken belt. A two-dollar replacement later, and I've now got two working machines, one for each floor of the house.

My first impulse, faced with a broken appliance, broken machine, broken anything, is still to start over, and start shopping. It's in my nature, it's in my genes, and the phrase "let's open 'er up" just generally doesn't fit anywhere in my vocabulary.

But recently on my trips out to the garage I've been looking with a mixture of sorrow and regret at the old canister vacuum which predated the other two, and just quit working one day. It sits, rusted now and covered with dust, waiting for a day when I've got the energy to lift it into the garbage can and set it out with the rest of the trash. Part of me keeps thinking about it lately, wondering if it was consigned prematurely to the dustbin of history because all it suffered from was "a broken belt" and I had simply lacked a more masculine gene of deconstruction and mechanical optimism.

I don't think I really want to know.

Back in the Saddle

The coastal breeze on Sea Island carried a bouquet of aromas. The tang of salt sea air from the Atlantic coast nearby, the lush marshes beside the causeway, palmettos, white gardenias in full bloom. But it was the familiar fragrance of horse hide and fly spray that hit me like a gentle glove across the cheek and made me smile and inhale deeply in recognition.

I was about to go horseback riding on the beach in coastal southern Georgia, and this was a very big deal for several reasons. Despite owning horses for close to thirty five years, I hadn't been on board more than twice in the last fourteen, ever since the riding accident.

I'm a very lucky person. I took a long fall off a tall horse in a jumping lesson when I was pushing my limits in more physical ways, and ended up in a body cast for three months with a fractured vertebra in the middle of my back. Every day, I remember how fortunate I am that I came out of the accident alive, and came out of the body cast hurting... but still walking. The accident was one of those transforming events that divides the world as you know it into "before" and "after." I got braver, I got more intuitive, I went to law school and tested my limits in ways I could never have imagined before. When you start law school with a severe tendency to hyperventilate when called on for public speaking, what are the odds you'll not faint from nervousness when you have to argue before the state supreme court? Pretty slim. If anyone had placed bets, they'd have a nice little nest egg now.

But the horseback riding, which had been part of my life since I was a pre-teen, fell to the side. At first it was a case of still recovering from the accident. I went for a whole year afterward, measuring just how much pain it would cost me to pick up a dirty sock, and keeping a running tally of the number of times I could reasonably bend over in a day before my back quit holding me up. And then I started law school. My theory at the time was that as my kids got older, they would need me less and I'd have more time to devote to school and other things. Any parent of high schoolers who participate in sports would have laughed his or her head off at my naivete. I found that as they got older, I only got busier...but by then it was too late to rethink the plan.

But free time was only part of the problem. As my body gradually regained some semblance of "normal," I found that by that point my horses had finally grown too old and decrepit with age to ride. One suffered from arthritis, the other from emphysema and the occasional case of "founder." They lived out the rest of their thirty-plus year lifespans as expensive and pampered lawn ornaments, their nearness a comfort and a thing of beauty but their "useful" lives done with as far as remotely earning their keep.

I climbed into a saddle only twice after that. Once was a trail ride a few years after the accident, with my eleven year old son and a group of other children who had taken some basic riding lessons through the local recreation department. This, I thought, would be easy. A nice, gentle, completely supervised reintroduction to a part of me that I truly missed. I confess I was scared to death the entire way, uneasy in the saddle, hestitant and unsure. The next time was a few years later, when I took one of my daughters out West for a trip before college. A trail ride through the woods near the Grand Canyon seemed like fun, we thought. Again, I remember an overlay of dread and not much else.

But here I was, staying down on St. Simons Island, Georgia, taking part in the "Scribbler's Retreat" writers conference, and visiting my favorite place on the planet with a whole new perspective. Recalling wonderful week-long spring vacations on St. Simons when the kids were all young enough to get the same Easter breaks, I had wondered, before I hooked up with the conference, whether I would ever have a reason to return to this serene place. And how it would feel to walk the beach solo, without a herd of four children to count heads on continually, like a mother duck checking her trailing brood.

I settled in just fine. Picked up a rental car for a day of "me" time before the conference started, sat on the beach beside a tidal pool and watched a Great White Egret move in stop-motion as he stalked his dinner, admired the last of the blooming azaleas in the area, climbed to the top of the lighthouse, shopped for souvenirs at a delightful stained glass shop, "Pane in the Glass," which had been completely off the register for me before despite driving past it dozens of times on earlier trips with the kids in tow. The same way someone leading a bull by the nose would be reluctant to take him into a china shop.

And in reclaiming myself on the island, I asked my island friend Jeanie to set me up with a horseback ride on the beach. No better place to confront the fears of the past, I thought.

And so here I stood, as the trail steeds rested in their shaded stalls, all freshly groomed and saddled and sprayed for the first ride of the day, steadily munching their hay and smelling like a familiar trip through most of my life. I was matched up with a well-mannered little chestnut mare named "Penny," and once we were properly cinched up and our stirrups adjusted for length, our little band of four riders and a guide set off at a leisurely walk to the shoreline.

I ached in various places for pretty much all of the two hour ride. Knees, ankles, thighs, hips—all were body parts that hadn't been shifted into this position on a regular basis since I'd started having kids. Twenty some years ago. But the rhythm felt good, and the morning sunlight on the ocean was beautiful, and for the first time since the accident I could say that I wasn't afraid.

The ride triggered a sea of memories for me. Weekend riding lessons with my aunt in grade school; Friday evenings spent cantering through the woods on the outskirts of Chicago with my friends in our high school riding club; lunging my buckskin in large circles with voice commands, a long-handled whip cracking the air gently behind his haunches for encouragement; Sunday mornings spent on trail rides when I was eighteen, worshipping at the altar of nature with just my favorite livery horse for company.

It was a delightful trip through banks of memories, and it's still far from over. And it all started with the smell of horsehide and fly spray...

Double Chocolate Lab

Bandit nearly bought the farm the other night, and it was his sweet tooth that would have done him in.

Bandit is a chocolate lab, eleven and a half years old, with chronic liver problems, a golf-ball sized cyst on his shoulder that the vet doesn't want to remove because of his age and the bad liver...and that's just the tip of the iceberg. This dog of mine—my fourth since I was sixteen—was a stray pup at an animal shelter when the kids and I brought him home eleven years ago. I joke that he must have some beagle in his background because he "sings" on occasion. Most often in answer to the question "do you want to go out?" This absolutely mystifies my boyfriend, who can't get the same answer when he asks Bandit the same question.

He's lightening fast, and still as playful as a puppy on the days when age doesn't come knocking on the door, and he's had separation anxiety bad enough when he was still new to the family that we put him on Prozac. No kidding. We also tried aromatherapy. It didn't work either.

But what's really made things interesting in the past few years is his taste for eating stuff that he shouldn't. Post-winter yard-cleanup can be such an archelogical excursion. After the snow melts, there's plenty of evidence of misdeeds laying in the grass. A half box of Kleenex scarfed down in boredom, still brilliant white after its trip through the dog. Fourteen sticks of chewing gum stolen from my purse recently… including the silver foil wrappers. The list goes on.

Chocolate—generally acknowledged to be poison when it comes to other dogs—needs to be kept under lock and key. My sons and I could have skinned Bandit alive a couple of years ago when he found the chocolate we'd brought home from Germany in our suitcases…and ate it all, leaving colorful wrappers in foreign languages all over the living room. Just a couple of months ago he polished off a carton of Nestle Quik on the front stairs, leaving nothing but a large chocolate stain behind. Never an ill effect for the dog, though it tended to leave the humans in the room pretty steamed!

My kids and I have long ago learned to keep our bedroom doors closed behind us at all times because of other behavioral …quirks. But the other night, my youngest son fell victim to juggling too many things at once—violin practice, then tennis practice, and a violin lesson after the tennis practice—and forgot to shut the door behind him before he left for the night at his dad's.

I got home from work and didn't notice. Drove into town for an hour's worth of errands, and came home to find the paper wrappers from two huge Cadbury chocolate bars my son had brought back with him from Scotland as presents for the family just the week before. The chocolate was nowhere in sight. Bandit lay on his bed in the kitchen, with a very guilty look on his face. "Bad doggie," I said, and went to town again to meet some friends for a wine-tasting. I didn't even bother to shake a finger at him. We've reached an understanding over the years. He's going to do something he shouldn't, and I'm not going to like it.

Two hours of delightful conversation and a lesson in how to mix peaches pureed in sugar syrup with Italian champagne for a "patio drink" later, I returned home at nine to find to dinner plate sized pools of regurgitated chocolate on the living room carpet (off-white of course) and a very sick doggie. I shooed him outside to keep being sick and miserable, then Googled chocolate+dog+poison. What I found scared me plenty.

We set off for the animal emergency room twenty five miles away, where Bandit was X-rayed, his stomach monitored, an IV line run to pump him with fluids, and some charcoal somehow inserted down his gullet to absorb what chocolate it could. By the next day and $550 later on my credit card, I had a healthy dog again, along with the memory that I had run a quick cost calculation of what I could possibly afford to spend on an eleven year old dog with a bad liver (nothing, if you really must know!) and ultimately checked the "do not rescuscitate" box when asked what should be done if he went into cardiac arrest. I hope nobody tells him. I'm sure he wouldn't have checked the same box for me! But the last time I took a dog to an animal emergency room, I spent $3,700 dollars on last-ditch surgery...and he still died the next morning. It took me years to pay it off. I knew I couldn't afford to do it again.

Bandit's back to normal right now, which means chewing on sticks in the yard and following me around with a tennis ball in his jaws, hoping I'll throw it. The only lasting markers from our adventure are the dark circles under my eyes, the shaved patch on his foreleg from where the IV was inserted, and the chocolate stains on the carpet. I've shampooed them four times now and figure on leaving them for the carpet cleaners some time between now and Thanksgiving.

My son was suitibly apologetic and deeply chagrined over causing the whole incident by leaving his bedroom open and the chocolate available. He informed me that there were actually three Cadbury bars in his room. They're all missing now. One was probably wolfed down with the wrapper intact. I'll find the evidence some day when I'm out in the yard.

In the meantime, I figure all that guilt's gotta be worth some really good help with the yardwork this summer.

Toolbox Therapy

 There many ways I deal with stress. The chronic, day-in, day-out variety like the splendid and noble insanity that comes with working in a prosecutor's office, usually calls for chocolate. On a regular basis. Cops and co-workers have even been warned on occasion to not approach unless they're bringing some good chocolate to feed the beast.

Other spikes in adrenaline or responsibility have been dealt with by buying yet another pair of spike heels. Lime green with perforations, magenta suede with patent leather bows, leopard print brocade slingbacks, I can tell you a story behind nearly every pair of stilettos in my closet.

And yet another favorite release is to escape to the shoreline of my favorite state park on Lake Michigan with a soy mocha with whipped cream from Starbucks and bury my hands in soft white sand as seagulls and sandpipers look on, unmoved. That has been a luxury untouched for a long time. The annual state park pass on my dashboard is two years old.

But right now, neither chocolate nor shoes nor nature will do. I want a clean, functioning bathroom. My father is dying in a hospice and my youngest child is leaving for college in a week, and an imported chocolate bar with hazelnuts is just not going to cut it.

Reclaiming and repairing the bathroom is symbolic, there is no doubt. I've been juggling family emergencies from insane distances for months now, and in the past few weeks the carpets in the house have grown another layer of cat hair. The carpets are oatmeal. The cat is black with long hair that never stops shedding. My kitchen and dining room are awash in paperwork related to the complicated business of getting old and navigating medical issues and applying for public benefits, a fitting payback for a long life spent dutifully paying taxes.

And I don't just want a routinely clean bathroom, I want it gleaming. And so the other day I brought the step-stool up from the basement, went to my maximum fear-of-heights two steps and unscrewed the four frosted glass shades and chandelier bulbs from the brass fixtures above the sink and washed them with soap and water for the first time since they were installed. I think that was about ten years ago. The dust around the edges has been bugging me for a long time. A feather duster only gets so much.

Today, in between visits to the nursing home where my father lingers in hospice care, I decided to tackle the sink. It's a two-basin sink, with fittings of brass and white porcelain that resemble upside-down tulips. Remodeling the bathroom about ten years ago, with fresh flooring and a cherrywood cabinet, was a major bone of marital contention for several years leading up to it. The green-light for the remodeling project came, unfortunately, too late to save the marriage. But I ended up with the house in the divorce, and so I've still got the lovely sink and the cherrywood cabinetry. The cold water handle in the sink I use, however, has been getting looser and looser for the past couple of months, and today, with an empty house and a few hours to myself, I tackle the project.

Only one of the two sinks actually works anymore. Several years ago something went seriously wrong—the kind of "wrong" you actually call a plumber for—with one of the sets of faucets. I couldn't find an exact replacement anywhere. And so, loathe to replace both sets of pretty porcelain tulip faucets, I suggested swapping one set for the other. Because of the bathroom layout, nobody ever used the second sink anyway. The plumber cannibalized what he needed from the working side of the counter and shut off the water supply to the sink less traveled.

To my optimistic eye today, it looked like another round of cannibalizing was in order, this time swapping one handle and screws for another. It had to be done sometime. I could envision the handle falling off in my hand some morning as I was brushing my teeth. I took all the junk off the counter, wiped it down, and grabbed the smallest screwdriver I could find from the collection in a ceramic planter next to the kitchen sink. I don't know why I have a bunch of screwdrivers sitting there next to my birdwatching binoculars, they date back to the early days of marriage and full-time motherhood when screwdrivers just sat wherever my ex-husband decided to put them.

Now, more than twenty-five years later I look at the ugly yellow ceramic planter and think "I should do something about this." But in the meantime, as pathologically disorganized as I am, I know I can at least find four things in an emergency—my car keys, my cell phone, clean underwear, and a screwdriver.

Unfortunately, this turns out to be not a job for a regular screwdriver, which I discover when I insert the screwdriver in the first tiny hole relevant to the project and start to turn ("lefty-loosy, righty-tighty"). I grab my huge floating boat flashlight from the closet—okay I can really find *five* things in an emergency—and take a closer look. I don't have a boat, by the way, but I love these flashlights. For about five bucks at the hardware store you get something that could pretty much light up a stadium on a foggy night...***with the battery included!!*** And they're so big they are impossible to misplace.

What will be required here, I discover, is a tool called a "hex wrench." And I actually, believe it or not, own one. Since the divorce I have gone out with a couple of men who liked to impart knowledge of some of the mysteries of "the man zone," and as a result I can now use a cordless drill, appreciate the necessity of draining the water heater once in a while, cut firewood with my pint-sized chain saw, and hang a picture. One of my favorite mottos is that a girl can never have too many box-cutters.

The intricacies of a hex wrench were first explained by the man in my life, the guy with the longbow and the motorcycle and the black leather pants, when we needed to disassemble and then reassemble my wrought iron bed a couple of years ago for the carpet installers. It is a weird folding tool comprising many small metal rods that fold into a sheath like my Swiss Army knife (okay, now we're up to finding *six* things in an emergency!). I pick the smallest prong, which is not much bigger than a toothpick, and get to work loosening things that seem to be important. The screws that awkwardly emerge are about the size of peppercorns, and I can foresee absolute disaster if I drop one of the four down the drain. Who invented these things, I wonder? My hands are tiny, with chickenbone fingers that wear a size four and three-quarter ring, and I can't imagine how men with much bigger hands ever navigate these contraptions for a living.

And yet I persevere, and swap the wiggly faucet handle for the tight one, and with one miniscule crank at a time I feel a sense of control, and satisfaction, and pride, and finality, and closure. I snap the metal prong back into the casing, under the larger wrenches, and think that I'm *glad* I know how to use a hex wrench. And that I have my own tool kit. Even though it's technically a fishing tackle box, picked because of its lovely color scheme of turquoise and translucent white plastic. It's nice to get rescued some times, but it's nice to fix your own household problems once in a while too.

The bathroom looks just lovely right now. I haven't put all the hair supplies and toothpaste and makeup and perfume back on the counter just yet. It's too pretty a sight to mess up just yet with the mundane. Later in the day I'll be back en route to my father's bedside, a helpless spectator in a play which I have absolutely no control over. My son will be leaving the nest not long afterward, creating a void I have no idea how I will fill.

But for right now, at least I can walk into the bathroom, look at the sink, and grin.

Back Away From the Bunny

It's the dog days of summer, and that can mean only one thing.

It's time to go to the fair.

I've been to two this year so far, the county fair and the state fair. Marvelous opportunities to people watch, eat food on a stick, pay way too much for alcohol, weigh the relative merits of things you'd never make at home like deep-fried s'mores, deep-fried cookie dough and chocolate covered bacon, and traverse the midway looking for more and more inventive ways to spend $20 to buy a stuffed animal worth two bits. I spent only six bucks this time, coming out ahead of the average, using a mallet to pound a catapult flinging a succession of rubber frogs into a barrel with rotating lily pads, and winning a tiny white stuffed tiger which I promptly surrendered to my boyfriend's daughter. She's eighteen. What, I should keep the toy for myself? My traditional prize-winning duty done, I passed on any further opportunities to win goldfish, throw darts at balloons, toss basketballs, fling plastic rings at upright soda bottles.

Because for me, the fair's not about the games, the food, even the music. The essence of a fair on a hot summer day is ... the animals.

Oh, the black and brown Clydesdales gleaming like dark satin under the floodlights in their jingling ten-horse hitches, silky white "feathers" floating around their hooves like cheerleaders' pompoms as they thunder around the coliseum, tons of beribboned and disciplined muscle on the hoof. *Oh,* the incredible assortment of chickens, some weirdly resembling poodles, other looking like eccentric characters in a British barnyard comedy. *Oh,* the cows, spotless and brushed and shampooed, nearly odorless, chewing contentedly in their stalls surrounded by perfectly clean straw, while the calves nestle together as cute as a basket of puppies. Sigh... I could go on and on and on.

It's not like I haven't seen cows before. Or horses. Or chickens. Or rabbits.

Over the years, I've been in the position of living with and cleaning up after all of them, in ways that left lasting impressions. At seventeen and Chicago-bred, I'd been privy to an abundance of bovine company when living on a once-working farm with my family in northern Wisconsin. Call it a social experiment gone awry, for a few years we nonetheless packed our decrepit barn with a horse and some ponies and some calves and some geese and some chickens and ducks and a pig. Noah's Ark meets Green Acres. The barn swallows moved in on their own.

When it came time to milk the cow my parents brought home from an auction one day, I was the only person brave enough or stupid enough to step up to the job that evening with a bucket between my knees and a wooden stool to sit on. We named her "Queenie," and the two things I remember most are the fact that she came with some wicked-looking horns ... and she didn't like to stand still during milking. The stool didn't have wheels. It was quite the sight, watching me scoot on my little stool to follow her, the milk sloshing back and forth in the pail, and quite the job twice a day.

But milking was by far the friendlier task. What goes in must go out, and after hauling bale after bale of hay into the barn and shaking it out in front of Queenie's nose, I recall shoveling mountains of ... by-products ... from the trench behind where she stood into a wheelbarrow and out the back door of the barn to a large, fragrant heap. A lot of what I was doing back then fits in the "character building" column. I've been told that I'm quite the character.

Likewise, when it came to the two horses I owned for more than thirty years. Yes, I just loved to look at them in a summer pasture, their tails switching back and forth as they grazed, their ears swiveling like semaphores at every sound. The sight of a horse grazing in the sunlight on a warm summer day can still make my heart skip a beat in fond remembrance. But again ... I was no stranger to cleanups, and medications, and fly-repellants, and near-death experiences at night in freezing barns, and hauling heavy hay bales and fifty-pound sacks of horse feed around.

But the animals at the fair—they're like what Playboy centerfolds are to real women, what Marie Antionette's little hobby farm at Versaille was to a working farm in the French countryside. For the rest of us, not the hard-working exhibitors, these are eye-candy! Fantasy animals! Hollywood groomed and ready for their close-up, Mr. DeMille!

Really, what little girl or boy watching the Lone Ranger and Tonto thunder across the mesa in pursuit of bad guys ever thought that Silver and Scout might throw a shoe? Or need a hay wagon following somewhere behind in the badlands? Was there ever a pooper scooper mentioned in an episode of Lassie? Did Wilbur ever lift a shovel behind Mr. Ed?

So with that frame of mind—voluntary and total suspension of reality—I stepped into the fairs. Oooohhhed and aaaaaaahhhhhhed over the flashy Clydesdales stepping smartly with their jingling harnesses. Chuckled at the chickens, cooed over the newly hatched baby chicks. Debated where, on a "cuteness" scale, human babies fell in relation to puppies, kittens, and fuzzy ducklings. (The jury's still out on that one.)

Walking past the dairy barn at the tail end of the evening, I passed by a lovely Brown Swiss heifer placidly chewing her cud. She was spotless, she was dust-free, she could have stepped right out of a Gainsborough painting. My arm immediately crossed over the low wooden fence to stroke her neck, and in an instant I was enveloped by the smell of fresh hay and memory and in some ways much simpler times. My hand found its way up to her ears and her forehead, and the recollection of just where to scratch to make a cow happy came flooding through my fingers. The heifer leaned into it as I worked my scritching around the nubs of her horns and around the base of her ears. If cows could purr, this one would have sounded like an Evinrude motor.

It was a delight. Still, when I go to the fair, I know I'm in no danger of acting on impulse and bringing home a horse or a cow or a goat or a camel. The rabbits, however, are another story.

For decades of fair-going, the rabbits have been among my favorites to look. So soft, so plush, so cuddly looking, so clean, so touchable! Blank slates of fluffy goodness. I did, in fact, succumb the siren song of cuteness a few years ago. Wandering past rows of "Mini-Rex" rabbits, my oldest daughter, soon bound for college, stared longingly at a perky brown rabbit that looked like the Velveteen Rabbit come to life. "Oh, if I was going to have a rabbit, that's the one I'd want," she said.

About three weeks later, we had a rabbit living in a crate in our kitchen. Yes, he was **extremely** cute! But she left for college about a month later, and for the next three years reality hopped around on my kitchen floor with inevitable surprises. I think we could have weathered just about anything else, but this bunny came with, ahem, personal hygiene issues that were truly dispiriting. I think that if someone had invented bikini waxes for bunnies, he might still be with us. But eventually, the routine of giving a fat, kicking rabbit haircuts in unspeakable places proved to be one too many things for me to juggle at the time, and he was routed to the local humane society, along with all his gear, food, crate, litter box, yogurt treats and toys. The cat has since taken over his job of covering all surfaces in the house with gossamer fluff.

And yet...I felt that dangerous surge again this year as I dawdled past rows upon rows of rabbits in their cages, clean, odorless, non-threatening, fluffed and brushed and fed, with ribbons displayed proudly beside their name tags. Nary a rabbit dropping to be seen underfoot. No hygiene issues here. The pull was magnetic, nearly tidal. I could feel common sense fall away at the possibility of owning one of these lovely, cuddly little animals again. I could feel myself falling in love-at-first-sight all over again—that ridiculous moonstruck phase that never really lasts but fires that brain chemistry to dizzying heights nonetheless.

I shook my head and forced myself to take a step back from the cages. Focused my mind not on the bunny in front of me but the one that had hopped around my kitchen for three years, leaving deep scratches on my arms every time it was bath time at the kitchen sink. Recalled litter cleanup and bunny hair tickling my nose and the necessity of running interference between a six pound rabbit and a sixteen pound cat. I stepped out of the small animal barn and back into the sunlight. I had escaped!

There's one more fair to go to before the end of summer, and so I'm not out of the woods yet. Looking into the rabbit cages, for me, is like an alcoholic staring at a bottle, or Elizabeth Taylor staring at Richard Burton. Oftentimes surmountable, but sometimes not.

I just hope that next time, I'll continue to conjure some common sense to balance out the endorphins and optimism that no doubt will start up all over again. And if I can't, that whoever I'm with will just take me by the arm, give it a tug, and say...

BACK AWAY FROM THE BUNNY!!

Objects in the Rear View Mirror...

The news of his death was nearly four years old, but it was still news to me.

Earlier that day I had appeared in court for a routine set of "initial appearances" on some criminal cases, and had smiled to myself at how closely one of the defendant's names resembled that of a boy—a young man, really—I had gone to journalism college with. It had been a good fifteen years since I heard from him in the aftermath of a college reunion only one of us attended, brief updates changing hands via email. He had become an acclaimed newspaper reporter in his field, had married, and he and his wife were eagerly awaiting the adoption of a daughter from China. He sent me a copy of a recent award-winning series he'd written to bring me up to date on his work. I can't remember if I returned the favor.

I promised myself that I would look him up when I got home after work and shoot him a quick email about the morning for a shared laugh. But while I waited on "hold" as a polite, drawling young police officer in Alabama searched for some information on an individual I had charged closer to home, curiosity got the better of me and my fingers quickly typed his name on Google.

I hit "enter" with a quiet confidence, expecting to find the name of his most recent newspaper employer and, hopefully, an email address. What popped up on the screen instead was an obituary. And the news that his death nearly four years earlier had been "investigated as a suicide." The smile of anticipation turned to the taste of ashes.

Thirty years passed away in an instant, and I felt both hollow and tremendously sad.

My mind kept turning back to younger, more innocent days, when we all shared the shining idealism of young journalists in the post-Watergate years. Dustin Hoffman and Robert Redford had made investigative journalism seem not only rigorously principled but absolutely *glamorous* in the film version of "All the President's Men" just a couple of years before. Nobody told us we couldn't change the world every day, and even if they did, we wouldn't have believed them.

The young man I remembered was tall and slender, with gorgeous deep brown eyes and the broad shoulders of a swimmer. We were never very close, but our journalism school was small, and everybody pretty much knew everybody else. I remember that he was unfailingly polite, and well spoken, and ferociously smart. He was a couple of years younger than I was, at a time when things like that mattered, and he had what I think of as "Breck girl" hair—layered and a bit stylishly long and shiny and squeaky clean. He cooked dinner for me at his apartment one evening—one student-apartment building over from where I lived with my roommate—and I remember a night of baked pork chops and candlelight and glasses of wine and nice conversation. We shared a G-rated kiss in his doorway as I left to go back to my own apartment and reality.

I printed off a bunch of pages about his passing, and read them the next day, parked down at the lakefront under a cold, sunny sky. There were so many things I had not known. There were profound and well-earned accolades by the dozens, fond reminiscences, tributes to his inspiring and encouraging nature, celebrations of his colorful character and incredible intellect. But along the way there had evidently also been depression, professional turmoil, a strange admission years earlier that he had slept for a while with a gun under his pillow.

The thing which had apparently tipped the balance for him to take his own life beside his favorite fishing spot, it was reported, was an upcoming initial appearance in court on a charge of drunk driving. The sort of thing that is absolutely routine for me on the other side of the table, but in his position obviously terrifying and unfathomable. I guess it's true, that "the bigger they are, the harder they fall." I tried to put myself in his shoes, tried to imagine how he must have felt at this very public frailty, his reputation as a crusader for the public good on the verge of being seriously tarnished, and the humiliation that would have followed. It didn't feel too good.

As the days passed, the shock finally lessened. I tried to "shake it off," rationalizing that we had never actually been close friends, that I shouldn't feel this so personally. By the next time I had to appear in court for more "initial appearances" in drunk driving cases, I was back to my usual form, confidently asking the court to require this, that, and the other thing as bond conditions "for the protection of the public." It's my job, it's what I do without hesitation and without doubt.

But in the moments in my office when the phone isn't ringing, when nobody's looking for my signature in a hurry, and I've caught up just briefly with the tide of paper that drives my work, I can see him still. Tall, slender, in blue jeans and a checked shirt, standing at the top of the stairs outside his apartment, smiling, his eyes a beautiful brown, and the light from the hallway shining on his fluffy "Breck girl" hair.

Pelican Lessons

Everybody's got "the story."

For some folks—most famously Oprah these days—it's the "aha moment," that wonderful instant in the cosmos when a vital, incredibly important, life-changing realization strikes and the heavens part and the world divides into "before" and "after" and the path ahead becomes suddenly clear.

Before the "aha moment" entered the modern lexicon, it was the "Eureka moment," inextricably linked to Archimedes jumping out of his bathtub a couple of millenia ago and running naked down the street with excitement at the recognition of the concept of water displacement, which was—and still is—a very big deal.

Well, "aha" and "Eureka" moments are great and all, but there's something beatific and divine and let's face it, bland and rather undramatic about them in the long run. I think "aha" and I think celestial energy and light flowing down from the heavens to shed enlightenment without irritation or effort or sweat or rueful discovery.

The story I'm sure everyone has lurking in their past and marking another important fork in the road has a bit more of an edge and a definite learning curve to it.

I think of it as the *"I knew it!!"* moment. It's that flash of genius when you realize that you've been listening to the wrong voices (sometimes your own), ignoring your own insight and intuition, turning a blind eye to the truth. It's that moment when a wife's discovered her husband was in fact cheating and the lipstick on his collar really wasn't hers; the good advice of friends wasn't nearly as good as it seemed; and that little old lady who lived down the lane really *was* running the drug ring you suspected but just couldn't put your finger on why, or get past the smell of her gingerbread cookies wafting into the street as you passed.

The "I knew it!!" moment sometimes comes with a tinge of regret, often comes with a "once bitten, twice shy" moral, and always comes with the conviction that listening to your inner voice is the most important counsel you'll keep from now on. It can appear while you're laughing out loud, crying with disappointment, or having coffee with a tart-tongued buddy. And despite our best intentions, if we're slow learners, we can even get more than just one.

In my own case, I'll admit to being denser than a gourmet cheesecake at times and I have several of these road markers along the way. The most portentious, serious, highest stakes incident involved ignoring that "inner voice" in favor of taking one more run at a wood fence on a tall horse against my better judgment, and ended up with an ambulance, lights and sirens, a backboard, a whole lotta pain, and the words "you have a broken back" to ponder for the following three months in a body cast.

But I'd rather not use that reference point most of the way, when all I really need to think of are...pelicans.

The road to revelation was a two-lane ribbon of asphalt that ran through the Horicon Marsh. I was passing through on a long drive from the courthouse where I work to the University of Wisconsin-Madison where my daughter was receiving an award of some sort that came with a very nice dinner. With no time to spare, no binoculars or field guide in the car, and no hiking clothes either, I still stole ten whole minutes to explore a three mile driving loop through the marsh that caught my attention as I drove the scenic route recommended by a cop I work with. So I'd rather watch birds than people. Sue me!

I drove deep into the marsh and far from passing traffic, and parked the car by a boardwalk that ran directly into the marsh. I stepped into a world of water and nature and trilling sounds and wonder. As the late afternoon sun shimmered on the water and illuminated the tall vegetation beyond, there were myriad takeoffs and landings occurring around me, splashings and wingbeats and fluttering sounds. Something white caught my eye, and I stared in wonder as three huge white birds soared in from the periphery and came in for a landing past where the glimmering plane of water was interrupted by rushes and cattails and an air of mystery.

I stood, transfixed and mesmerized until they disappeared. The golden sunlight shown on gleaming white feathers with wingtips tipped in inky black. From my far-off vantage point, there was a joy and and an ease and a lilt to their flight as they circled and floated and finally landed gracefully in the reeds, well protected from prying eyes. These birds were huge. They seemed the size of hang-gliders, easily the biggest birds I'd ever seen.

And there was a flash of something familiar to them. For just an instant, I thought "pelicans!!" And then reason and rationality set in and I shut that thought down. "Nah," I thought. "Couldn't be." Too big by far, entirely wrong in color, a thousand miles from the Georgia shoreline where I was used to seeing them skimming the waves and the palm trees overhead like prehistoric throwbacks before alighting by the dozens on a sandbar in the Atlantic.

I got back in the car, drove the rest of the way to the awards dinner, and wondered all night and for days after what exactly I had seen. Could they possibly be whooping cranes? I knew that a few of these rare birds had been sighted recently somewhere in the marsh, and that seeing them was like finding the birdwatcher's Holy Grail. Could I have been among the chosen few?

I pondered the mystery for the next few weeks. Called a Department of Natural Resources warden I worked with on occasion and asked his advice. Where had I seen this trio, he asked. We weren't entirely sure that the area of vegetation was a customary place for whooping cranes to nest. Had I thought about the possibilities of trumpeter swans, he wondered. What about herons?

I stewed over the puzzle for weeks, reaching out to other birdwatchers with little satisfaction. The optimist in me really hoped that I'd seen a trio of whooping cranes. What an accomplishment!! What bragging rights!! But as I thumbed through my well-worn bird guides, I realized that this couldn't be the answer. Whooping cranes would have the same silhouette in flight as the slightly smaller sandhill cranes I could identify in my sleep—a vaguely alien form, as though you took a goose and added an element of elastic to it, neck strangely thin and elongated, long legs trailing out behind like twigs. I'd caught just a fragmentary glimpse, but there was an elegance of movement that could not be denied. Just like a few bars of Beethoven's **Für Elise** can be mistaken for nothing else.

Likewise for herons—the size was off by a lot. What I'd seen was enormous. And the more I looked at the descriptions and listing for trumpeter swans, the more I recognized that the flight pattern was wrong. The birds I'd seen soared and glided and flew with a playfulness that swans and geese, I knew, just didn't have. If you've ever paid attention to a goose in flight, you know that it's a big-ass bird. There's a lot of meat to haul from one point to the next, and there's no room in that equation for burning fuel to have fun. A goose reminds me of a C-130 transport plane—it moves a lot of weight, and flies in a no-frills straight line.

I had reached a dead end. The mystery was still alive and well, but I was all out of leads. I tried to push it out of my mind.

A few weeks later, though, I was back at the marsh, this time for a leisurely morning of hiking and bird watching, a sanity break in a busy life, a battery recharge at the font of nature. Sneakers on and binoculars looped around my neck, I walked, and I sat, and I kept an eye out for another glimpse of those white visitors. No luck. As I finally heading home I took a different route, one that ran past the wildlife refuge's main visitor center. I stopped in, looked around, stepped out on the deck and looked out at the marsh spread out before me. A ranger was working in the office, and I put the puzzle to her. Explained the inspiring thrill of the sighting, the inquiries, the ponderings, the frustration.

"I'll bet they're white pelicans," she said.

WHAT!!!

Unbeknownst to my local expert fifty miles away, the Horicon Marsh is a summer breeding ground for thousands of white pelicans. I hadn't even known they existed. I'd simply asked the wrong person for advice. The ranger showed me a postcard in the gift shop. Sure 'nuf, they looked right. I ripped through my bird guides to the section on pelicans I'd never thought to open, and there it was, in black and white and full color. With a wingspread of nine feet, no wonder I'd thought they were the biggest damn birds I'd ever seen.

And with that, I smiled, even laughed a little. "I knew it!!" I thought in triumph.

And now as I blunder through every day since then full of judgment calls and leaps of faith and decisions big and small, if I need a little validation for the idea of trusting my gut, I just look back at a warm spring afternoon on a Wisconsin marsh, and think...

Pelicans.

Magic Words

I learned a new set of magic words today.

We all have our repertoire of magic words and phrases. There are the ones that are drilled into us from the time we're old enough to talk, namely "please" and "thank you." Then, as we get older and get a little life experience, we learn a few more. Like "no thanks, I'm driving." And who can forget Homer Simpson's sage advice to Bart, "it was like this when I got here!"

Sometimes magic words are completely dependent on the surrounding circumstances. "Previously diagnosed with heart failure" will get you farther up the list for a second opinion with a cardiac specialist than, say, "sale on Jockey underwear in aisle four." The words "oh my god, my water broke!" will get you more helpful attention in an emergency room than they will, say, standing in line to buy Springsteen tickets.

The magic words I learned today are *"I'm the mother of the bride, and I'm looking for..."* In terms of getting me quickly to my destination, it was on the scale of Moses parting the Red Sea.

This discovery came about when I set sail this morning for Bayshore Mall in Milwaukee, with but one goal in mind—finding some suitable evening wraps for the bride and her three attendants before my daughter's outdoor wedding in two weeks. Somehow in the hubbub of testing out caterers and bakeries and fabrics and dresses, we'd overlooked that detail...and September in Wisconsin can turn a wee bit chilly in the evening.

A pocket full of discount coupons for Boston Store in my pocket and a vague idea of two or three stores located in the mall that I could try, I parked the car in front of one well known women's store, strode in purposefully, and made my pitch to the first sales associate I met.

She knew just what I needed, and immediately found the only dressy silk wrap in the store. On sale. With another twenty-five percent off. We bagged it up in case this was "as good as it gets," and I put some more money in the parking meter and continued on down the street.

The next few stores yielded a mixed bag of results. One had the seemingly perfect thing for all four girls—washable soft woven wool wraps in a rainbow of colors—for fifty dollars each. I took notes and kept shopping. The next two had nothing just right...but two of the sales associates at one put their heads together and came up with the names of two youth-oriented stores I would have never thought of trying. And the convoluted directions of how to get there from their sales counter.

I bought a few pashmina wraps that were perfect at the first store they suggested, then just for fun and due diligence, walked into the other and made my "I'm the mother of the bride" announcement. The sales girl knew right off the bat that her store didn't have what I was looking for…but shared that she'd been recently been shopping for something similar for a wedding of her own, and found it in the scarf aisle of Boston Store. She even thoughtfully told me which cosmetic counter would be the polestar of my navigating. And she was right.

I left the mall with a one bag of four pashmina wraps and another as a spare, as well as a few "trophy" items for myself. (I can't possibly walk into Talbots during a summer sale with a $25 gift certificate burning a hole in my pocket and walk out empty handed!!) But the most astounding thing was finding out the wonderful effect that the "mother of the bride" announcement had on people. It was a phenomenal discovery, the key to cooperation and collaboration and pleasant conspiracy on a scale I'd never experienced shopping before.

I think my wedding acquisitioning is finally done, at least for this particular daughter. But there's something about using those marvelous new words that makes me want to trot them out and summon the magic all again.

Maybe after the wedding…

Disconnected

It was one in the morning, and I was completely disconnected.

The sliver of a moon had long set, and above me was a solid black sky studded with more stars than I had ever seen. The Milky Way drifted like a gossamer scrim across a swath of inky eternity, and Jupiter rose over a nearby tree, shining like a beacon. A large chorus of bullfrogs sang in the distance. Theirs was a primitive, wordless music, which started with a few isolated twangs like a rubber band. Then, as if a froggy conductor stepped up to a stump of a podium in white tie and tails to direct the orchestra, a deep and steady ***thrummmmmmmm***, and then silence. Then, after a few measures of relative quiet, the twangs signaled the orchestra's warm up again.

We were on a long weekend driving trip to see friends in Michigan, and I hadn't checked my email in three days. Or seen a newscast, or read a paper. It felt weird…and wonderful. I wish I could have said the same thing about my cell phone during this trip, but with four kids to keep tabs on as well as elderly relatives faltering more by the day, that was out of the question. But just now, at this hour, even the phone was turned off and left behind in the house.

The place where we stayed was in a rolling area of southern Michigan known as the "Irish Hills." Two days earlier, and only a few hours into the trip, our frenzied and frustrated pace had vanished as soon as we rounded Gary, Indiana, and decided to ditch the bumper-to-bumper construction-delayed traffic crawling on the interstate in favor of something more rustic...and moving faster.

Our first official nod to "vacation time" was a stop at the Indiana Dunes National Lakeshore, where we parked our folding chairs on a sandy beach and ate the sandwiches I'd picked up from Panera Bread at 7:30 that morning. The wind was stiff and cold, and the waves were high. Seagulls hovered in anticipation around our feet and lurked just over my left shoulder until we finished lunch, leaving them no leftovers. I took picture after picture of the park's pavilion, made of intricately patterned red brick and faintly Moorish detail. I took the wheel for a while, relearning how to drive a stick shift. I killed the engine a good dozen times at various stop lights, and added another fifty miles to the drive when I missed a road sign as I was struggling to put the Chevy into first gear again...and again.

We took the meandering old Chicago Road that had begun as an Indian trail, and turned into the main pre-interstate route between Detroit and Chicago. Or—around two hundred years ago—the primary military transport road between Detroit and Fort Dearborn. The two-lane road now ran through tiny towns with names like New Buffalo and White Pigeon, and was lined with houses that wore their age gracefully, with gingerbread flourishes and deep shady porches and lush hanging baskets filled with petunias. "For Sale" signs abounded... as did occasional pockets of commerce.

It was a land of few McDonalds but any number of one-of-a-kind restaurants, and a handful of drive-ins as well. We ate burgers and fries and Cokes at one, and I rued the fact that there were no tailfins on the little silver Aveo. As soon as we'd placed our order, the radio station started playing something by the Beach Boys. And then Martha and the Vandellas. And Gary Puckett and the Union Gap. We sat in a time warp as we scarfed down our meals.

In the three days we escaped from routine, we canoed on a series of quiet, sleepy lakes, making our way through flotillas of water lilies. The only sounds that surrounded us were bird calls and the occasional slap of lily pads against the sides of the boat. We went to a backyard barbecue, played a seriously competitive game of beanbag toss, ate at Harold's Diner, took in a rodeo, just sat around.

We would be leaving early the next morning, with more than three hundred miles to drive to get back to our daily lives. The Chicago Road would inevitably have to give way to holiday traffic on the Indiana and Illinois Tollways. And I'd eventually have to sit back down at a computer and connect with the "real" world.

But the evening air was cooling fast, and the sky above was absolutely hypnotizing. I pulled my folding chair closer, and rested my head on the soft leather jacket covering a familiar shoulder. As the bullfrogs periodically gave their throats a rest, a bunch of coyotes chimed in and howled in the distance. Fireflies sparkled brightly, illuminating the drift of fog rising from the lake across the road.

And as I nestled in and looked up at the stars above, I felt completely... connected.

Marley & Rocket & Me

I just got over weeping through the end of the movie, "Marley & Me." My youngest son had bought it on DVD for his sweetheart, and the two of them were all settled into the sofa with me for a routine Sunday dinner-and-a-movie night to start the week. They'd seen it. They loved it. They thought I'd love it too. It caught me by surprise.

Let's stay straight off that it's a marvelous movie. A lot deeper and richer than I'd expected, having only seen the movie trailers, which were heavy on the slapstick and nonexistent on the character development. I even knew that **spoiler alert here if you've been living in a cave for the past year** the dog dies at the end. Hey, I'm a firm believer that "all dogs go to heaven." It's an okay ending for any dog movie. You get to picture them up there romping in sunny, celestial fields, gnawing on a rawhide bone or chasing a fuzzy yellow tennis ball that never gets dirty or wet with saliva.

But what I didn't count on was the fact that not only did this incredibly destructive yet beloved movie canine look *exactly* like one of the best dogs I'd ever had…he died of exactly the same thing. It had been twelve years since I'd wept like a baby at the unexpected passing of a dog who drooled like a St. Bernard, slouched like a lion, and stood as tall as a pony. But there I sat on the sofa with two happy but mystified teenagers, surrounded by damp Kleenex, voice cracking and sobs lurching and gasping from my chest, explaining that unlike Marley's owner in the movie…I never got to say goodbye.

Rocket was the third one of my string of uniquely wonderful dogs. Muttsie came first, a beagle/dalmatian mix who strayed into my life, attacking our flock of Leghorn chickens one day when I was home alone on the farm. She sported one brown and one icy blue eye and a combination of spots and patches that made her look uncannily from some angles like Adolph Hitler. She was mine for fourteen years, and the phrase "dogging her master's footsteps" was invented for this dog. Shadow came next, a purebred Flat-coated Retriever with a glossy, silky long black coat and magnificent physique, and a stark deficit in the brains department. In nine years despite the "retriever" in his name, he never learned to let go of the tennis ball he brought back to you for another throw. He wanted to wrestle you for it instead. I'm a quick learner—a game of "fetch" always started with two balls. The boys grew up using him as a shared pillow while they stretched out on the living room floor and watched cartoons. Shadow loved to run around with a stick in his mouth…though at a hundred pounds, the "stick" could be a tree branch and when he ran up joyfully behind you and accidentally whacked you with it as he flew past, you felt it for a while. If you were still standing.

Shadow eventually passed on after nine years, and there was a four-footed void to be filled. I've never known life without a dog, and I believe deeply in bringing kids up with a canine companion. I look at dogs and see furry, tail-wagging, divine packages of unconditional love. They don't hold grudges, they forgive you everything, and they are always happy to see you. Take two kids growing up in parallel universes—same houses, same yards, same schools, same friends— but give one of them a dog. I guarantee that the kid who has a dog has a richer life. So not getting a new puppy was never an option.

We found Rocket nearby in the neighborhood, one of a litter of gorgeous yellow pups produced by a union of a prim and proper purebred Golden Retriever and a randy neighborhood lab who just didn't respect boundaries. Word of warning for folks relying on a buried electric dog fence—it'll keep your dog in the yard, but it sure won't keep the other dogs out!!

The kids fell in love, and we brought Rocket home as soon as he was weaned at eight weeks. We "crated" him in the kitchen at night, a training tool that had worked well with Shadow as a puppy on the theory that dogs inherently like enclosed spaces where they can retreat and feel safe. This little guy, however, deeply (and loudly) mourned the sudden loss of his mother and siblings, and I spent the first three nights lying on the kitchen floor next to his crate to keep him company. By the end of the first night I figured that if I ever got another puppy at eight weeks, it would kill me. On the up side of things, I saw some truly beautiful sunrises.

The little guy started to grow like Clifford the Big Red Dog. He hit twenty pounds in just a few weeks and got too big to comfortably carry in my arms. Damn!! He kept on growing, and by the time he was six months old he stood tall enough to look over the kids' shoulders at their breakfast cereal on the kitchen table. I swept the contents of the middle kitchen counter to someplace else, and bought a few bar stools so that the kids could eat their meals at a higher dog-free altitude. So life's full of adjustments. We had the perfect dog! He romped, and fetched, and cuddled, and just plain lazed with us without impatience. He was another of what I think of as the "hundred pound club," but tall and rangy. He had grown into his puppy paws that had looked at the time like they belonged on a lion, and he slouched around the yard with a grace that was absolutely feline, accentuated by an extraordinarily long tail that carried and twitched like a big cat's. He was the size of a pony, with a deep chest and a deep "woof" and a tawny coat that reminded me of Elsa the lioness in "Born Free."

For the first time I could remember, we had a problem-free pooch. No tendency to wander off like Muttsie, no fondness for chewing on us and the furniture and the cabinets like Shadow...Rocket was good-natured, and lovable, and well-behaved, and housebroken, and above all, cuddly. Maybe if we'd had him longer this honeymoon phase would have worn out. But after only a year, we would never get to find out.

He seemed suddenly in distress one night, wanting to go out repeatedly, unsure of what to do when he got there. In the circle cast by the yard's floodlight, I noticed that his sides seemed oddly distended. It was nine at night, but I called the vet and described Rocket's symptoms and appearance. "Don't even bother to bring him here," the vet advised. Take him as quickly as possible, he said, to an animal emergency center in Milwaukee, thirty miles away. This was serious.

We packed a layer of blankets into the back of the minivan, settled Rocket in, and I set off on a desperate mission. I'm sure that the statute of limitations has run on speeding tickets from twelve years ago, and these days with the job I hold I'm sworn to uphold the law and the Constitution. So let's just say vaguely that if there had been a cop that night equipped with a radar gun as I flew past edging close to triple digits, I would have been in big, big trouble. The expressway was virtually empty, though, and Rocket and I made it to the clinic without incident or arrest.

He was unloaded, and examined, and the diagnosis was that he had suffered a "gastric torsion." In other words, his stomach had twisted in that deep ribcage of his, cutting off the blood supply to his intestines. Surgery was an option, but it was expensive and most dogs would not survive anyway. What did I want to do? I pulled out the charge card and authorized a preliminary look around. The news was bad, one of the worst cases they'd dealt with. What did I want to do? I called my husband. Could we afford this? We took the charge card out again and said "go ahead." I spent part of the night at the clinic, part of it catching a few winks of uneasy sleep on my friend Judy's sofa in Milwaukee.

By morning Rocket had made it through $3,700 worth of surgery, and I stopped by the clinic to see him before heading home. He was bandaged, and hooked up, and looked like he'd been through a hell of a lot. But he was young, and incredibly strong, and as I stroked his head before leaving, I felt sure that he would turn out to be among the small but lucky percentage of dogs who could survive this. I would have stayed longer, and held him more, but my younger son's birthday party was set for that morning, and in another couple of hours a dozen little boys would be showing up in our backyard to paint a "teepee" made of scrap lumber and scrap bedsheets and put on little feathered headdresses and run around noisily and eat hot dogs and scarf down birthday cake.

The clinic called about twenty minutes before the first guests arrived. They were very sorry, but Rocket hadn't pulled through. I blinked back tears and told no one the news as I put on a headband with a blue feather myself and went out to greet the guests and their parents. Two hours later, the party was over and it was time to drive back down to bring home our dog.

I brought my oldest daughter with me. It was a silent drive to the clinic. We couldn't claim Rocket right away. The clinic was bustling that morning and we had to wait our turn. We sat side by side as dogs and cats and their owners came and went. A big yellow lab sat directly across from us, beside his master. Black, liquid eyes, golden coat, sturdy shoulders just asking to be hugged. My eyes started to mist up. Beside me, I could hear my daughter fight back a sniffle. We looked at each other, then back at the dog. I caught his owner's eye, and made a special request. Our dog just died…and he looked exactly like yours. Could we pet him please? The lab's owner graciously said yes, and we wrapped our arms around our new friend, who stood stoically as our tears fell and dried on his yellow fur.

Rocket's buried in the yard, with a lilac bush to mark his final resting place. In the movie, Marley's spot is marked with some large rocks, but I like the idea of something growing, and blooming, above my old companions. Muttsie has a lilac bush of her own, and Shadow rests beneath a rose bush.

I don't think I could possibly watch "Marley & Me" again. But for the first time in quite a few years, my mind is again enjoying the memory of a big, friendly yellow dog who graced our lives and passed much, much too soon.

The Romeo and Juliet song

There's a guilty pleasure I just have to confess. And then explain.

Not that there isn't already a list. Belgian chocolates. High heels. Coastal Georgia. Guys in uniform. The movie "Gladiator." Tropical drinks with little paper umbrellas. Down pillows and flannel sheets…as long as the air conditioning is still on.

But this is a chapter, and a phenomenon, all its own.

I'm a grown woman over forty…and I like the Taylor Swift song "Love Story." There I said it. Out loud.

You know the song. You can't possibly escape it on the radio. It's the one where she's Juliet and he's Romeo and it's got pre-feminist-to-the-point-of-Neanderthal lyrics like "Romeo save me…"

Good God, I thought, the first dozen times I heard it...or heard enough of it to change the channel with a cringe. How utterly **dopey**! How ridiculous. How unreal. How...godawfully uncomplicated and fairy-tale and unconnected to the realities of love and relationships. And for heaven's sake, didn't anyone read to the end of the Romeo and Juliet saga and realize that the star-crossed lovers **died??** So much for teenage romance!

So that would be the starting point of the journey to actual affection. Active dislike, morphing into something else. Just like real life. Or any number of romantic movie comedies, such as "You've Got Mail." Okay, Tom Hanks and Meg Ryan had a lot to do with making that one work, but still...it's a formula for romance on the big screen. Even Harrison Ford got to be loathed by Anne Heche in "Six Days Seven Nights"...and nobody doesn't like Harrison Ford.

It was the beat that caught me first. Rhythmic and pulsing and steady and smooth (relentless, even), like the slap of a long plastic jumprope on a sidewalk during summer vacation. Three girls killing time on a warm afternoon, the jumper in the middle always changing, the rhythm as consistent as crickets chirping. Equilibrium as perfectly maintained—despite the occasional shift in positions—as a gyroscope spinning on a picnic table. I found myself humming along, even after I changed the channel. And then I quit changing the channel altogether, and looked at it through a new window.

Everything that drove me nuts about it at first—especially the cloying fairy-tale neediness of it—became a window into being a teenager again. Back in the day when all you could see was what you wanted, absolutely, with all your heart, right now, with no thought for the future other than the credo that love could conquer all.

Remember those days? Mine, I'm sure, were fueled by a childhood spent reading too many romantic suspense novels full of dukes and other noblemen waiting to rescue their damsels in distress and whisk them off to a life of happily-ever-after. It took me years to outgrow that template.

Well, by the time you've passed thirty-nine, you've grown up and figured out that no matter how grand love may be, it doesn't always conquer all. And it certainly doesn't get the toilet fixed or the living room painted or the dog taken to the vet. Real life is full of real frustrations, big and small, and tender eurphoric feelings sometimes have to get put on hold for just a wee bit of time while you run into the corner gas station to buy a carton of milk. Because you just can't live on love all the time…groceries and utilities and clean laundry are usually involved too.

But…

I've realized that when I listen (and even…*ulp*…sing along to) "Love Story," I don't have to think about real life at all. It takes me right back to being sixteen and absolutely blissfully ignorant of the myriad disappointments and compromises that real life will offer later. By the time the song wraps up with "Romeo" on bended knee telling our heroine to go buy a wedding dress because he loves her and that's all he needs to know…I get a quick fix of bottomless yearning fulfilled and a "when dreams come true" instant that's about as real as the Disney version of Cinderella, and just as much fun. Reality be damned for just a minute!

And as I've learned just not that long ago, those magic moments aren't entirely lost when your teen years are left behind. I had one of my own in the middle of a gardening project at my house with a man whose pickup truck and leather tool belt and love of blooming things beat out any central casting figure of a prince on a white horse.

One Sunday morning, after the plants were in and the mulch was spread and green things were watered and beginning to take root, the subject came up over coffee of how to create a footpath through the flower garden, which was rather deep in places. I, cursed with character flaws of ambivalence and a pathological fear of commitment and absolutely no imaginary sense of the visual, balked at every suggested solution. Hedged, even, at the idea of going window shopping. For rocks.

So we took the truck out to a local quarry anyway just for something to do, with the fig-leaf of understanding that there were always supplies for his own place that he could buy and therefore it wouldn't be a trip wasted. We walked, hand in hand in the sunshine, over pretty displays of granite and marble and slate and bricks. And when we reached a stretch of red Arizona sandstone, I could suddenly see my heart's desire. And imagine it among my flowers.

I still hemmed and hawed, pricing it out, trying to figure what I could afford, wondering at the enormity of the project, wondering whether I should go back home and think on it for a while longer. Like another week or two. And then Prince Charming cast his two cents into the pot, roughly rounded up to the fact that this was exactly what I wanted, we had the truck with us, it was a gorgeous day, and we might as well go for it.

I still remember the joy bursting in my heart as I threw my arms around him at that point and kissed him in the sunlight somewhere between the limestone and the crushed lava, casting caution to the wind and simply saying "yes!"

As blissfully simple and momentarily satisfying as the ending in "Love Story"?

You betcha!

Love in the Time of Cupcakes

The last of the "tennis ball" cupcakes set sail this morning, a small but telling harbinger of the fact that I'm going to be facing an empty nest in the fall. Twenty seven years of "hands on" mothering symbolically reduced to two dozen clumps of devil's food cake in little foil baskets. They swooshed out the door with my youngest son, for what would turn out to be his last tennis meet of high school. He graduates in another couple of weeks, heading for college in the fall and instantly turning any use of the words "high school" into the past tense.

I've been making cupcakes decorated like tennis balls—light yellow frosting with the slightest tinge of green, arced with curves and swoops of white icing—for fourteen years now, ever since my oldest daughter signed up for high school freshman girls tennis before the school year even started. Call me OCD, I don't mind! I consider it a badge of honor.

111

There are fundamental differences between "girls tennis" and "boys tennis" and only some of them have to do with testosterone levels. Girls tennis season starts in late summer and continues barely to early fall, guaranteeing splendid and warm afternoons and entire weekend days watching budding young ladies flit around on the court in bouncing pony tails and miniskirts, suntanned legs flying. Girls tennis, from my experience on the sidelines, has involved matching hair doo-dads with color coordinated ribbons, team posters, lots of conversation, and a great appreciation for cute snacks. Hence the tennis ball cupcakes, a big hit for both my daughters and their teams for a bunch of years.

Boys tennis, on the other hand, starts just on the cusp of very early spring, when winter hangs on for dear life. And here in the upper Midwest, winter's claws are deep. More than one tennis season for my sons has started its first practice as snow flakes were falling. The weather leans more toward rain, and cold, and wind, and if there's coffee involved for blanket-wrapped spectators under grey, stormy skies, it's been hot, not iced. Very few boys sported pony tails, and nobody wore matching barettes. The guys still appreciated the cupcakes…but I don't know that they even noticed the decorative flair right before they inhaled them.

And still, despite the fact that for years my cupcakes have been nearly vaporized in haste (and without a single squeal of how "cute" they were) by their entirely masculine patrons, I clung to tradition. At least once a season I needed to send those sweet, fluffy treats along to a meet, even if, as the years went by and my job schedule got less flexible, another tennis mom would actually have to deliver them for me. Call me crazy, it's been done before.

While the tennis ball cupcakes stretch back fourteen years, the cupcake thing has actually been a fixture for something more like twenty four. Long ago enough that my oldest daughter would have needed to bring a birthday treat for kindergarten. Or preschool. So through the next two and a half decades, the miniature confections were a constant and a comfort amid the multi-tasking, crisis-response mentality that goes into raising four kids with a minimum number of trips to the emergency room. There were cupcakes with sprinkles for birthdays, cupcakes with candy dots for art shows, cupcakes decorated like little ghosts and jack-o-lanterns for Halloween.

This last tradition—the Halloween cupcakes—nearly drove me into the ground once. I had three kids in the same grade school at the same time. The youngest wanted Halloween cupcakes for his second grade class party. I signed on for two dozen, half of them orange and half of them white, with little ghost outlines and pumpkin smiles drawn on with melted chocolate, eyes made from chocolate chips. Then the fifth grader chimed in. I signed on for another two dozen. And then as I started the baking, when I thought of my daughter's class in eighth grade going without my cupcakes on this festive day, I threw caution to the wind. Halfway through decorating seventy two little ghosts and jack-o-lanterns with dribbly chocolate I rethought my enthusiam... but it was too late to turn back.

I was planning to dress up for the second graders' party, and I tweaked my daughter with the thought of showing up in costume to deliver the goods. She's got a dark, sultry beauty to her, and she warned me off. "Mom, don't you dare!!" she said ominously, her eyes flashing like the fiery gypsy in **Carmen**. I filed that thought in the "hmmm..." pile. Made some soothing mention about bringing a change of clothes.

The next day I dutifully and precariously loaded six dozen cupcakes into the minivan, and set off for school. Fifth grade cupcakes were dropped off and put out of mind. The second grade Halloween party was so cute it could make your back fillings hurt. I think that was the one where I'd made my son a little royal blue cape with fake ermine collar, for his part as the "king" in a teeny tiny little play.

And then the lunch bell rang. I grabbed the last two dozen cupcakes from the van and walked them down the length of the school to my daughter's eighth grade classroom. As I stood in the doorway, her back was to me. A friend she was chatting with looked up, and announced slyly, "Sarah, your mom is here." Slowly she turned… and there I stood, a shallow cardboard box filled with treats utterly overshadowed by my appearance in a Pocahontas style beige fringed tunic with red embroidered trim, black leggings, and a feather in my hair. I bit back a grin, but it was **really** hard.

My daughter flashed daggers at me with those dark brown eyes. If looks could have killed, I'd be writing this from the great beyond. But at the same time, despite her fourteen year old peer-reviewed fury, I could see the corners of her mouth start to turn up in a smile in spite of herself, at the sheer **perversity** of my guest appearance. I delivered the goods and quickly exited stage left, fighting back a laugh.

Eight years later we were chatting on the phone as I drove to drop off yet another batch of tennis ball cupcakes for her younger brother's meet the next day. I was going to have to miss this contest too, and so once again the cupcakes were going to stand in for me, making me feel like I was still sharing a part of the adventure. We shared a good laugh about the day I showed up looking like Pocahontas at her eighth grade classroom. At the age of twenty-two, you develop a lot more perspective and forgiveness for antics like that.

I bemoaned the fact that with her in college, I didn't have the opportunity to bring festive or seasonal or downright ridiculous treat to her classes anymore. "Mom, you can bring cupcakes to my class any time!" she assured me. "We'll eat 'em!" I could resist pushing the envelope. If it was around Halloween, could I wear the Pocahontas costume again? There was just an instant of hesitation, then... "okay!" I could just imagine her eyes rolling across the miles between us. Maturity comes in many forms, and learning to humor a mother during a fleeting moment of insanity is a remarkable milestone for a daughter of any age.

I never did drive eighty miles to a college classroom after that to bring a sugary treat to a bunch of accomplished and sophisticated college students. Life just got a little too busy, it seems, though in hindsight I wish I'd grabbed the opportunity. But I still remember laughing at the memory with her, and the beautiful thread of give-and-take the offer and acceptance held, binding us tightly and preciously with love and affection despite the distance.

They were just cupcakes. And then some.

Rabbit Season

 Under identical circumstances, the pet rabbit would have shredded me.

Smokey, the sixteen-pound scimitar-clawed, white-fanged scale model of a perfect predator on the African veldt, lay stretched out on my lap, belly up, front paws draped comfortably over my forearm and the rest of him spreadeagled to the ceiling and limp as a rag doll. Trust is not a problem for this big fella, and as a CNN anchor droned on about the latest in presidential politics, my other hand wielded a sharp scissors, snipping bushels of long hair from his chest and belly and parts south. Among the first things to go, the bushy Charlie Chaplin pants billowing out from under his tail. A sensitive area, you would guess.

While I think professionally shearing this shaggy cat like a sheep to cope with shedding season would seriously mess with his head and his self-esteem, Smokey had been leaving black tumbleweeds of discarded fluff behind him everywhere he walked for weeks. He looked like a small bear stalking through the living room…or a furry ottoman. The man in my life had long ago suggested using his shop vac on the cat as a solution…but I could imagine the screams and bloodshed to follow. No, the surreptitious use of a scissors once in a while worked just fine.

I couldn't help but look back at "the rabbit years" with ironic appreciation.

We've been "horse people," "dog people," and for the past three years, "cat people." But somehow I don't think we ever made the grade as "rabbit people." Not that we didn't give it our best shot.

Our entry to the rabbit zone started, as most things do, with a massive amount of naivete, overlayed by a surplus of good intent.

The kids had always been suckers for anything small and furry. Childhoods passed with regular trips to state fairs and county fairs, with always a stop at the small animal building to laugh at the chickens that looked like oddly shaped angora rabbits, and the huge rabbits that looked like footrests with ears. At every juncture with a small pet— hamsters, gerbils, chinchillas, guinea pigs—the question always came up, "can we?"…and the answer was always "NO." I was in no hurry to add one more four-legged creature to take care of, and their dad was positively, deathly allergic to cats. We were damn lucky to have a dog.

But one year, a few weeks before my oldest daughter left for college, we drove a couple of miles down the road to the county fair, and made the annual pilgrimage to the small animal building. We laughed at the chickens, kept clear of the geese, found our way over to the rabbits… and then infatuation struck. The college-bound kid looked into a small cage at eye-level, locked eyes with a young short-haired rabbit, and breathed, "oh, look, if I was going to have a rabbit, that's the one I'd want."

We peered closer. She'd picked well. He was exquisite. Not much larger than a Fannie May Easter bunny, and a plush chocolate brown. He looked just like the Velveteen Rabbit, come to life. The inevitable question popped up. "Can we get a rabbit?" And this time, I just said "hmmmm....." And this time their dad didn't say anything. Big mistake. As I've said before, nature abhors a vacuum.

It was nearly a done deal from the start, contemplated through a happy haze of optimism and ignorance. With the kids getting bigger and no toddlers to chase after, how much extra work could this be? And of course, there was the absolute cuteness factor. And the oh-so-soft-to-the-touch factor. And the fact that I still get all misty eyed reading "The Country Bunny and the Little Gold Shoes."

Determining that this perfectly proportioned creature was a "mini-Rex," I quickly rushed in where angels feared to tread. If we were going to get a rabbit, it was imperative to do it before my daughter left for college, to give her one more cute, welcoming pet to remember… and come back to visit. I located some young rabbits at a breeder fifty miles away, and off we went. Passed over the two brown ones in favor of a white rabbit with grey Dalmatian spots. I recall him as having "more personality." My son remembers that the rabbit bit him on the finger. He came with a pedigree. He still got neutered.

Regardless, he came home and was installed in a cage in the kitchen, with shavings, and a litter box, and a water bottle, and a bunch of rabbit toys. And a half hour of recreation time out of the cage every morning while we were in the kitchen having breakfast. After much dismission, the kids finally agreed on "Zorro" as a name…and we never used it again. He pretty much answered to "here, bunny bunny!" and the promise of some yogurt-dipped rabbit treats.

The retriever didn't take the news well, though he wore his disappointment and sense of displacement with dignity. Having to share the kitchen with a small furry prey animal he should, by all rights, be chasing at sixty miles an hour across an open field, was a serious violation of the rules. He was still impeccably well-behaved, head resting on his front paws as the rabbit thumped his way around the kitchen, brown eyes following us and filled with reproach, ignoring the indignity. Though every once in a while, a sudden noise would cause the rabbit to bolt, and for a brief half-second the thin veneer of domestication would drop and Bandit would lunge at the primordial target, eyes flashing…until he remembered the rabbit was off limits, and sank reluctantly to the ground yet again.

If messing with the dog's mind was the only consideration, we'd probably still be "rabbit people." But for some ungodly reason, this particular bunny developed personal hygiene issues. He had packed on the pounds—he finally weighed in at six pounds, looking at rest like an enormous bunny slipper—and the zaftig proportions of Raymond Burr in his later years. And the end result was that he became a rabbit in need of constant bathing…and haircuts in unspeakable places.

There's a great Bugs Bunny cartoon from 1947, a Warner Brothers classic named "Rebel Rabbit," in which the world's most iconic delinquent bunny decides to set the world straight about just how tough he can be. Outraged by a two cent bounty on rabbits, compared with the $50 bounty for foxes and the $75 for bears, he mails himself to Washington and demands that the U.S. Game Commissioner explain the outrageous inequity.

"Well, other animals are destructive, harmful, obnoxious to people, they do damage. Rabbits are sweet, furry little creatures. They wouldn't harm a hair on your head," explains the clueless bureaucrat. "Rabbits are perfectly harmless, and the bounty stands at two cents!" That would, or course, be Bugs' cue to prove his point by striping the Washington Monument like an old-fashioned barber pole, cutting Florida loose from the mainland with a hand saw, and filling in the Grand Canyon.

The truth, of course, lies somewhere in between.

What I'd never realized before is that on the food chain, placement equals personality. Dogs and cats are high on the pecking order. They walk through their day secure in the knowledge that if they were kicked out of the kitchen and into the cold, cruel world, their job would be to kill and eat whatever they came across. That's why your cat may regard you as a fellow predator (and probably a far inferior one); and your dog may look at you as the leader of a hunting pack...but a rabbit is constantly looking over his shoulder, certain that everything he meets is out to put him on the menu. Relaxation isn't in a rabbit's inner lexicon.

Which would go far to explain why every time I wrestled the rabbit into submission and on to his back for a sponge bath or a trim, I ended up with a kitchen sink full of gossamer fluff, dirty, soapy water splashed everywhere, and long claw marks on my forearms, from elbow to wrist. The pleasure of his company began to pale a good year before we gave up.

The tipping point came finally when we bought the kitten. At two pounds, tops, Smokey ran from everything at first. He found the rabbit fascinating, but enormous by comparison. When the rabbit was loose in the kitchen, Smokey was perched safely on a kitchen chair, curiously watching this strange large creature thump around underneath him.

But then Smokey grew…and grew…and grew. By the time he weighed as much as the rabbit, I could see a possible conflict looming. By the time he weighed twice as much, the look in his golden eyes as he languidly draped himself over the seat of the kitchen chair spoke less of curiosity and more of sampling the menu.

A dream finally tipped the scales. I awoke one morning from a nightmare in which I'd returned at night from an out-of-town trip, to find the front of the house lit up by the flashing lights of squad cars and an ambulance, and crime scene tape around the house. In my absence, the dream went, the cat had murdered the rabbit, and the ceilings and walls of the living room and kitchen were drenched with blood.

I called the local Humane Society the next day. "Can you folks take a rabbit today?" They were open for business until eight, and within an hour I was there unloading the rabbit, his cage, the litter box, shavings, litter, toys, rabbit food, a bunch of those little yogurt covered treats… and a check for twenty five dollars. I drove away in the late evening sun, lighter by one rabbit, heavier by a massive load of guilt. It lasted several months before finally dissipating in a fog of other activity.

We still have a few reminders of our days with "bunny, bunny." Some chew marks on a gate in the kitchen. A handful of professional photos I'd had taken when he was still new to the family, pristine and untested and wonderously clean. A carrying case gathering dust in the garage. A picture I took around Easter one year, with the bunny sitting next to the retriever, and the retriever wearing white and pink rabbit ears. In the shot, the dog is licking his chops.

The only rabbit I see in my future now is the cottontail my son shot with his compound bow last fall in the backyard, dressed, and thoughtfully put in the freezer in a Ziploc bag. I still haven't figured out how to cook it, though Hassenpfeffer is right up there on the dinner choices, along with Colonial Rabbit and Rabbit in Tarragon Sauce.

Hmmm..... Maybe we're "rabbit people" after all.

Little Foxes

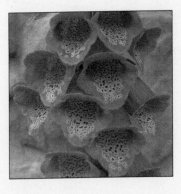

For the record, I was out in the woods hunting for a big rock. Not just any boulder, but one of mythic proportions. The "Bluff Headlands," the crown jewel in the county park of the same name in Door County. I had driven right past it the day before, evidently blind as a bat to its immense grandeur. I was taking another stab, this time with directions from a local. "There's a path that runs along the top of the bluff. Take it to the left, and you'll know when you're there!" he said with enthusiasm. A sucker for a pretty overlook, I took the bait.

Basted from top to toes in Deep Woods Off, I locked up the car and set off with a tapestry tote bag full of notebooks, pens and a camera. Figured on sitting and writing for a while once I located this most perfect place. In my mind's eye, I pictured a small-scale version of the Rock of Gibraltar in those old Prudential insurance ads. Bare rock face glowing in the sunlight, a beacon of solidity amidst the lesser, lower countryside. A spectacular view of the horizon from an immense height, with elbow room to spare.

I followed the first leftward path I found. It led jaggedly and steeply downward. I clambered and slid and grasped at tree roots and saplings to steady myself, trying to commit to memory the way back up. I ended up all the way down at the shore. It had felt like mountaineering to get there, and at the end of it I was as far from the top of the bluffs as you could get. But the view was gorgeous, and I had found both solitude and elbow room. I made myself comfortable on a rock slab, and basked in the scenery and the splendid isolation. It wasn't the Rock of Gibraltar, but it was beautiful nonetheless.

A pair of kayakers came past. "Have you seen the bluff yet?" they asked. No, I seemed to have missed it somehow. Go figure. They pointed back north from where they'd paddled. "Go back up and follow the trail along the rim. You can't miss it." I'd heard that before, but packed up and set out again. I scrabbled back up, trying to recall which slide of fractured limestone and tangle of mossy tree roots had marked "the easy way" down in the first place. I followed what looked like footpaths but proved to be dead ends, then retraced my steps and looked for another opening upwards. Climbing higher and higher, I finally homed in on what looked like the road less traveled, but still traveled a little. The path rose gradually, then leveled in equipoise.

Was I there yet? I thought so. There was a relative break in the trees, and the blue lake waters lapped at the shoreline far below, a tumble of rocks illuminated by the afternoon sun. Yes, this was a very far piece up from the shoreline! But here, a confessionary aside from your narrator. I love the woods, and I love being "up north." I find an incredible peace amid the lapping of waves along the undisturbed shores of Lake Michigan. But despite all that, here's a little-admitted fact of nature: after a certain point, it all looks the same. Cedar trees, pine trees, birch trees, branches tossing with white-capped blue water in the distance. Not unlike shopping for wallpaper—it's all pretty, but after one book one page looks a lot like another. There are many things in this world that have taken my breath away...but this exact spot wasn't one of them. Maybe it was more imposing when seen from a kayak bobbing on the water below. From where I stood, it looked more like a very long fall from a very tall cliff.

Still undeterred, and determined to make sure I hadn't missed the headlands a second time, I pressed on, noticing dimly that the path seemed to be going gradually down, and that it appeared to be close to vanishing altogether.

Shafts of sunlight broke through the canopy of trees ahead, catching my eye, and sudden movement stopped me in my tracks. I caught a flash of light gleaming off a tawny coat, and thought there might be a deer or two nearby. It was so much better than that.

One, then two, then three young foxes gamboled together in a small clearing, utterly unaware that that they had an audience no more than a hundred feet away. Identical in size, they jumped and stretched, flopped down in the grass beside a huge tree trunk, pounced on each other. They tumbled together ass-over-teakettle in a riotous tangle of tails and paws and ears and jaws, as fluid as a basket of kittens. White tail-tips flashed in the sunlight as they darted from light to shadow and then back again. They chased each other around trees and under deadfall, then sat, briefly apart, to take a break scratching their ears or their chins with dainty and fastidious grace. Then the game was once again afoot.

These weren't baby foxes, not like the wee bits of fluff that clustered around the paws of a red fox vixen who commandeered a woodchuck hole for her den in the back of my land a few years ago, all Disney-cute and comically helpless. They were nearly the size of adults, but still clearly in their first summer. They were more like "middle-school" size pups, practically grown up in size but with a baby-fur cast to their tawny red-gold coats, bellies full, an unguarded abandon to their full-tilt wrestling matches. Not for them the pinch-waisted silhouettes and hair-trigger vigilance of adults fending for themselves in a harsh world. As wild foxes went, these guys were almost…plump.

For a quarter hour I watched, entranced. For the most part I stayed as motionless as I have ever been without general anesthesia or really good sedatives. But I managed to sneak a few inches closer every time they were preoccupied with each other, or blocked by an enormous tree trunk between us. This was easier than you'd think. The ground was damp and spongy under my feet from the heavy rain the night before, and for the most part as quiet as a plush carpet. I slowly, carefully, let my bag drop to the ground and inched forward again.

Once in a while one of the kits stopped and looked straight toward me, and I stopped breathing and froze. In the shadowy part of the surrounding forest, dressed in dark blues, I must have looked convincingly like part of the scenery. I imagined myself as James Fennimore Cooper's fabled Deerslayer, making my way silently like a woodland wraith…and almost laughed out loud. My target was a snag of fallen branches just a few feet ahead. If I could just make it that far, I thought, I'd be content to sink to the ground, to just hide and watch for the rest of the afternoon. A few more inches, and the foxes played on, unaware. Another few inches, and I moved in slow motion. Almost there…and then with a snap of a branch under my foot, the foxes and the sunlight both vanished.

I finally found the "bluff headlands" two days later, with a third set of directions proving the charm. They were big. They were tall. And they were rocky…though not the Rock of Gibraltar. I suppose even the gateway to the Mediterranean looks more imposing from sea level. I sat on the bluff top and basked in the sunlight as long as I was there. A turkey vulture glided past, twenty feet below along the rock face. And the rustle of large wings and branches proved to be a bald eagle startled from his perch above me in a tree along the bluff.

But as I said earlier, after a few days in the woods, one rock looks pretty much like another. When I think of my quest to find the bluff headlands…it's the foxes I'll remember.

Makeshift Christmas

Imagination stood in for Christmas wrap this year.

"Sit down," I instructed my various children and my new son-in-law, "and shut your eyes!"

Then I exited stage left, grabbed their bundles of unwrapped presents from the spare bedroom, and returned to the living room where one after the other followed instructions and sat with eyes closed and hands face up on their lap to catch the goods.

"Okay," I said, "now just imagine there's a big bow! And shiny ribbon! And gorgeous wrapping paper, all sparkly and shiny! And when you tear that off, there's a box inside. Then you take the top off the box, and imagine there's some tissue paper! And you rustle it and rustle it, looking for what's under it, and finally..."

That's when I'd hand them their unwrapped sweater...or gloves...or flannel-lined pants...or scarf. We laughed, I got by without a nervous breakdown trying to find two extra hours for present decorating I didn't have time for, and there was no cleanup of tumbleweed sized balls of cast-off wrapping paper. I guess there's an upside to this after all.

It's been that kind of a Christmas. Never tried the "Emperor's New Clothes" approach to holiday wrap before, but hey, they say necessity is the mother of invention.

Two months ago I couldn't have foreseen that my eighty-five year old crippled mother would break her leg and need to go to a nursing home for three months, that my eighty-five year old father would need to follow her because of his own serious health problems, that my—*ahem, never mind how old*—godmother would suddenly wind up in the hospital only a month later in serious pain and distress, and that my father would then deteriorate suddenly and require hospitalization himself.

Two months ago I was still envisioning the kind of Christmas I wrote about two years ago in <u>Tale of the Christmas Axes</u>. The kind of Christmas that evokes echoes of Norman Rockwell with the seasonal decorations around the house and garland around the banister and the tree festooned from top to bottom with hand-embroidered ornaments and a glorious angel atop, a mistletoe ball hanging in the living room, family around the dinner table for a fabulous meal, Christmas music playing softly in the background. I'd even found the crèche this year that had been lost for the past two holidays.

But then life got in the way, and a few thousand miles got put on the car running back and forth again and again to my hometown of Chicago to deal with the unfolding dramas, and Christmas shopping and Christmas baking and Christmas planning and Christmas cards went right out the window. My younger son and I had managed to pick out a live tree a few weeks earlier and get it into the house and upright with the assistance of his lovely girlfriend, but with less than twelve hours left until Christmas officially arrived, the only thing the tree had on it was a few strands of lights. And bah humbug, I was about ready to leave it that way.

But somehow things went right anyway. By the time it was afternoon on Christmas Eve, the kids had come home and the ornament boxes got dragged out of the closet, and then some of our favorite decorations made it onto the branches through no effort of mine. While a new fire crackled in the grate, they then set to rolling out the batch of cookie dough I'd made the day before, and the usual irreverence and laughter and the smell of coffee lit up the kitchen as they came up with new demented ways to decorate the axe-shaped cookies and their "victims." Yes, we have Christmas stars and bells and pine trees and Santas. But we also ended up with a gingerbread man wearing a Speedo, a couple of Christmas giraffes, some Christmas pineapples, a pirhana, and a cookie decorated like a liquor bottle.

Then after the cookies were baked we raced through passing out my gifts before driving over to a family gift exchange, because I knew I'd be on the road to Chicago and back on Christmas day, visiting at hospitals and nursing homes and basically crashing my cousin's delicious family dinner on the way home. Not the best timing in the world, but it was the only day in the week that the weatherman could guarantee I'd have dry pavement and clear skies for two hundred fifty miles. I drove home in the dark to an empty house, since the kids had spent the day with their dad. Christmas dinner at my house is going to be a day late. I hope the chicken in wine sauce a few days ago is still good.

Taking inventory of this year, there are a few things we missed. The percentage of ornaments is a little thin this year...though the kids still managed to get the strands of wooden "cranberries" threaded through the branches. We're missing the angel and the mistletoe ball, the crèche never made it out of storage, and I can't begin to imagine getting out the garland. Never bought a wreath for the front door, left the big electric outdoor Santa down in the basement, and the singing moose that chimes "Grandma Got Run Over By a Reindeer" is nowhere to be seen. We skipped the tinsel on the tree too.

But we had warmth, and love, and laughter, and delight, and once again, Christmas cookies shaped like little bloody axes. As for the rest of the traditional things that got left undone, well...

We can always imagine them too.

The Vigil

The air streaming out of the grocery store cooler is dry and cold and bracing. I stand in front of an assortment of premium gourmet ice cream in single-serve cartons with high calorie counts and higher prices.

What flavor to buy for a dying man to coax him into taking a little more nourishment, a few more molecules of fat and sugar wrapped in the dulcet flavorings of Haagen-Dazs? Chocolate? He has quite the sweet tooth. Coffee? He loves his morning coffee. Dulce de Leche? Oh why the hell not? I buy two of each, then drive a few blocks further to a liquor store.

I am waging a war against death, and my pathetic weapons are ice cream, chocolate pudding and German beer.

It has been nearly a week since my eighty-six year old father, already afflicted by dementia and Parksinsons disease, was admitted to the

135

emergency room for the second time in a month with a perfect storm of converging handicaps—untreated diabetes, cardiac arrhythmia, a blood clot in his leg running from hip to knee, a raging bladder infection, and a foot in serious trouble from circulatory problems. Unable to speak articulately for months before this, he was unable to tell anyone the things going wrong in his body this time until they had reached critical mass.

He has now made it more than three days past the phone call from the hospital telling me—as I stood at the counter of a German gift shop buying him some more CDs of folk songs from his native land—that he would probably not live another half hour. This old soldier is tough... but he is still wasting away. He is now in hospice care, a method of care designed to ease suffering rather than aggressively try to change nature's course. Treating him with something even as simple as an IV line for fluids and nutrition has been complicated by his dementia—he has spent most of the past month in hospital beds with restraints to keep him from tearing the IV lines from his arms. A hospice worker who knows nothing of the man wondered aloud whether he had pulled his IV lines out because he wanted no further treatment to prolong his life. No, I retorted, given that he spent four years as a prisoner of war, three of them working miserably in a French coal mine, I think he was more likely simply trying to escape.

The conundrums are many. Enough pain killers and sedatives to dull the pain in his tortured foot keep him too sleepy to eat enough to regain some lost strength. Intravenous fluids would require readmitting him to a hospital and placing him in restraints again, which must be a horror to him. The difficulty he already has swallowing make it more difficult to get any measurable amounts of food or liquid into his stomach.

And yet…I know I have made small inroads. A half cup of ice cream one day. A half bottle of German beer yesterday, a full twelve-ounce bottle this morning, sucked down through a straw to the accompaniment of German soldier songs on the boom box. I knew I was on to something the day before when I lifted the straw to his lips and he tentatively drew in the golden liquid. Afraid that he might take too much at one time, I pulled the straw away. He tried to speak, and I leaned closer to hear. It was one word. "Again." Again what, daddy? More beer? Another single word answer. "Beer." I look into his hazel eyes that still light up sometimes with recognition when he looks at me, and I know I will keep it coming. There is no "bar time" at this place.

I feel helpless to change the larger workings of fate, and so I focus on the smaller things that I can do. A promise to bring some Bitburger beer, an evening ritual from a family reunion in Germany a few years ago. The collection of German songs, which he sometimes taps his foot to or tries to sing along with. I try to remember to wear bright, colorful shirts, and perfume, and long dangling earrings to catch the light. My boyfriend, who speaks a little Deutsch from his time overseas in the Air Force, sat with us and spun a tale of taking my father to Berlin to Oktoberfest. We set up a bird feeder on a shepherd's hook outside his window, and watched as goldfinches, bright as lemons, came to feed only minutes later.

I've brought my old chocolate lab to visit, tossing a bright yellow tennis ball around the hospice room to keep him busy. At one point I searched the room for the ball for another throw, but could not see it anywhere on the floor. It was only when I straightened up that I realized Bandit had placed it on my father's bed beside his elbow. I don't think my father knew this at all, but I still patted my retriever on the head in gratitude. "You're such a good dog," I told him.

This evening as I leave the nursing home I feel an inevitability settling in, a waning of hope. The odds are long against him.

And yet, as long as he's still breathing and still smiles at the sound of my voice, I will keep trying to fend off death, one spoonful of ice cream, one Oktoberfest beer at a time.

May it Please the Court

"May it please the court." The words are enough to strike terror into the hearts of most attorneys I know. They are the first words you speak when you address the Wisconsin Supreme Court in an oral argument. The words are ritual, as standardized and formulaic as Kabuki theater. And I was about to say them myself...if I just didn't faint.

I have a framed photo on my desk at work It dates from perhaps a year before I started law school at the age of forty, and only a few months before I would break my back in a riding accident, spend three painful months in a body cast, and have the world as I knew it divide into "before" and "after."

In the photo, I'm standing in a winter woods, with my four children gathered around me. They range, in that picture, from about three years old to thirteen. We are surrounded by pristine snow and bare trees, and framed in a pretty fieldstone archway. I am beaming, and my entire universe revolves around keeping them safe and warm and out of harm's way. If you had walked up to me then and told me that in just a few short years I would not only be a criminal prosecutor but find myself arguing cases before the state supreme court, I would have given you the same stare as if you'd told me a genealogical search had just revealed that I was really the Queen of England, and a Lear jet was standing by to whisk me back across the pond. Oh, and the roof at Buckingham Palace needs fixing.

I might have smiled pleasantly, rolled my eyes…and then called the police.

But fate—and a tall horse who steered like a barge—intervened, and barely a year after I was lifted off the sandy soil of a riding arena on a back board, my youngest son started part-time kindergarten and his mother started law school as one of the first part-time students enrolled at Marquette University Law School. I remember sitting in a large classroom during orientation week, surrounded by dozens of twenty-somethings young enough to be my children. An affable professor at the front of the room was demonstrating the Socratic method of teaching with an exercise that kicked off with the question, "who owns the moon?" I didn't really care about the moon right then, but as he spoke I felt an oppressive cloud of pessimism descend on me like a starless night.

What was I thinking? How could I possibly survive this, competing with kids who had no families and no pets and no responsibilities, who could close the law library and then go out for drinks and convivially debate legal theory over pitchers of beer, who could read textbooks with their breakfast cereal? In contrast, I had four kids, a dog, two elderly horses, and a marriage that was teetering on the verge of collapse. My sense of doom right then was as deep and all-consuming as a black hole.

But on the ride home, I reminded myself that I'd already borrowed the money for the first year…and I might as well show up for class the following week. I soon found a comforting road rhythm in driving the thirty miles to school, studied like crazy for four hours every Friday morning, kept ferrying children as usual to tennis and soccer and gymnastics and volleyball, skipped class whenever there was a field trip or it was my turn to be the "hot dog mom" at the grade school. And somehow, through it all, I managed to keep a decent grade point average.

There was one serious barrier for me to conquer, though. All my life I'd suffered from a tremendous, crippling fear of public speaking. Call it panic attacks, anxiety attacks, sheer nerves, I was unable to get up in front of a room full of people without my heart racing and my breathing going tight and shallow, and my voice starting to shake with dread. I will never forget the first time I was called on to "brief" a case in front of a law class. Standing near the back row of an amphitheater classroom, I could feel the cold wind of fear and desperation creeping up my back, and while I knew the subject well, I barely choked out the words. The professor sat, motionless, on the edge of his desk at the front of the room. I have often imagined what must have been going through his mind. Two questions, really. First, if I died of fright, what on earth would he tell the dean? And second, what would he do with the body?

After that first debacle, I forced myself to confront my demons. In every single class after that, I read ahead and raised my hand, determined to say something on point. Little by little, with every attempt, my heart quit pounding quite so hard, and my voice quit quavering so much. Still, it was a decidedly uphill climb. When the rest of my classmates showed up conservatively dressed in suits for our first mini "oral arguments" in a legal writing class, I showed up in jeans and a Mother's Day t-shirt that read "Best Mom in the Whole World." I wore it to remind me that if I fell flat on my face in school, I still had a life. If I had to do that day over, I'd still wear the same thing.

Three and a half years after I started, I finally graduated from law school with an honors degree and a commitment to finding a job in criminal prosecution. I was lucky enough to soon land a part-time position with the District Attorney's office in Sheboygan, Wisconsin. The post was newly created, and both my boss and I were open to suggestions on how to make the best use of my time.

As a former journalist, I naturally gravitated to writing projects— briefs, motions, research, appeals. And then one fine day one of the other attorneys in the office turned up at my desk with several pounds of paper for me to review. He had won a TPR ("Termination of Parental Rights") case at trial before a jury, but the judge had subsequently refused to terminate the parent's rights based on a technicality. What did I think?

I had been a prosecuting attorney for less than a year. I had never looked at the Children's Code before this. But I rolled up my sleeves, read the statutes and the judge's decision, and came to the conclusion that the judge had gotten it wrong. My boss gave me the green light to file an appeal.

A few months later, the written decision came down from the Court of Appeals. The appellate judge ruled in favor of the trial court judge. Once again, several pounds of paper landed with a thump on my desk. What did I think? We had now lost the case twice in a row… but when I looked at the law and the appellate court's reasoning, I came to the conclusion that **this** one was wrong too. I got another green light, this time to go knocking on the door of the state supreme court. The petition was granted. And I was absolutely terrified.

All of my old fears of speaking before an audience came flooding back, in spades. As a survival mechanism, my obsessive compulsive streak kicked in then, and I zealously over-prepared. Terrified that I might not have an answer, or that my mind might just go blank, I researched... and rehearsed...and researched some more.

The stakes were high, as they always are at this level of argument. On a personal level, the case came down to whether a three year old boy who had been placed in foster care for very good reasons could be freed up for adoption by a family who wanted him. On a broader plane, the issue that would be decided for this case and all cases coming after it was just when in the formal TPR process the courts should stop favoring a parent's right to stay connected and start considering the "best interest of the child."

Since the case involved a young child who clearly deserved a better life, the "mother tiger" in me kicked in as well and I spent weekends working on the case. I pulled over to the side of the road just to jot down ideas on Dairy Queen napkins that came to me as I was driving. I sat cross-legged on the floor of the courthouse basement, poring over dusty statute books from the 1800s, trying to trace the path in the law from when children were considered property to the realities of the present day. I rehearsed my introduction over and over again as I drove, afraid that if I didn't have the words absolutely committed to some subconscious part of my brain stem, I might freeze like a deer in the headlights.

And finally the day came to argue before the high court. I had brought my older son with me for company. I treated him to lunch beforehand at an Italian restaurant. I passed on his offer to share his breadsticks, and took another dose of Pepto Bismol. My friend and co-worker who had tried the case joined us at the court. As he sat beside me in the packed room, I told him "if I pass out, just pick up my notes and keep reading!" I wasn't kidding.

It was my turn to go first, as the person who had asked the high court to hear the case. The justices filed into the courtroom in their black robes, and solemnly took their seats. One of the justices and I had been reporters at the same newspaper many years earlier, and she gave me a quick smile as our eyes met. I don't recall that it made me feel any less nervous. As I began to speak, I could feel my chest start to tighten and my air supply go dangerously short. My voice shook for a bit, but it passed. I remembered that what was at stake was far more important than what I was afraid of, and my breathing finally returned to normal as the justices started to pepper me with questions about the case and the law.

Gratitude and relief beyond words flooded through me when I finally got to sit down and turn the hot seat over to the attorney on the other side. When the court was done with our case, my son and my friend and I left the courthouse and stepped out into the sunlight. As I cleared the doorway, I looked at the sky and declared, "Thank God I'll never have to do that again!!" I was absolutely sure that I wouldn't survive another go-round.

The three of us headed to a nearby restaurant for a little celebration. We settled in to our air-conditioned seats, and ordered drinks and nachos. As we waited, I repeated my heartfelt desire to avoid such an incredibly grueling experience again. My friend looked at me and smiled wickedly. "You know, I've got another case I want you to look at…"

Timelines for appeals in cases involving TPRs are mercilessly short. I wouldn't have thought it possible at first, but only five weeks later—and months before the first case was even decided—I had finished another brief and had it sitting in the supreme court's "in" box. And I got to prepare and argue two *more* cases to the court after that in the next couple of years. Then I finally got to catch my breath. Even now, the thought of saying the words "May it please the court" can make my heart race.

As for that first case...the decision eventually came down months later in our favor, 7-0. I like to say that the good guys won. But win or lose, every time I look at that picture from the snowy woods...I remember how far I've traveled.

About the Author

Mary T. Wagner's award-winning essays have been described in terms ranging from "barbed wire prose" and "the Midwest's answer to Carrie Bradshaw" to "bedtime tales for grownups."

An experienced journalist and criminal prosecutor living in Wisconsin, Wagner draws on her experiences as a newspaper reporter, soccer and tennis mom, truckstop waitress, radio talk show host, judicial clerk, office temp, and cocktail waitress to craft compelling stories of ordinary moments viewed with extraordinary insight.

She harbors the fond hope that someday she'll win the lottery and afford to become a "snowbird," trading brutal Midwestern winters for a seasonal warm spot on the beach in Georgia, a big bottle of sunblock, and a frozen strawberry margarita.